Stop Your Stinking Overthinking

Strategies for Quieting the Busy Mind, Letting Go, and Staying Present

Barbara Heavens

Table of Contents

Introduction

Author Fyodor Dostoyevsky (1864) once wrote, "Thinking too much is a disease," and I can't agree more! What's odd about it is it's almost addictive. Once you enter a cycle of overthinking, you get stuck there, and your brain keeps at that subject until it exhausts itself. Like having a popcorn kernel stuck in your teeth, it's irritating, yet simultaneously entertaining. The kernel's not good for you, but your tongue keeps toying with it. Likewise, the spiral of continuous contemplation is harmful to your physical and mental health, yet your mind keeps spinning it round and round.

Overthinking is aptly named. It occurs when you think about a particular thing over and over and over for long periods of time. You might venture a little sideways sometimes, but you never steer completely away from the main subject.

Like, it rained the other night at my house with lots of big lightning strikes and loud rolls of thunder. Well, my dog is scared of thunder. He has PTSD from a few years back when lightning struck one street over and broke a water main six feet under the ground. None of us humans were home at the time, so that had to be terrifying for him! So anyway, it was storming, and the dog was shaking. If anyone in the house moved, he'd shadow them and stick like glue to their heels. I picked him up to snuggle and comfort him, and that sent me down a rabbit hole of lightning strikes. I got to wondering how they worked and why they happened. I thought of photos I'd seen of spectacular hits that branched out in all directions. I remembered all the lightning rods on just about every building in a nearby theme park, and that got me contemplating the number of times those have been struck—the answer is many, by the way. All these ruminations were set to the words of an old Fleetwood Mac song that says, "Thunder only happens when it's raining" (Nicks, 1977), and that got me thinking, *Does it?* And so down that track I went, trying to prove Stevie Nicks wrong. Meanwhile, the storm passed, and my dog jumped down, but I was still sitting there, lost in thought, hearing thunder rolling in the distance but seeing no rain outside my window.

Some people believe overthinking is a good thing. They believe that if they think about a certain problem, situation, or conflict enough, they'll eventually find the solution. The opposite is true, though. The more time you spend pondering an idea, the less time you have to develop it and put it into action. On top of that, the longer you dwell on the topic, the less likely you'll be to accept any solution as the *right* one. So what happens instead is that you end up mentally and physically exhausted. Instead of, say, creating world peace, you deplete yourself of any semblance of peace at all.

Psychologist and author Dr. Susan Nolen-Hoeksema detailed the research she performed in her book, *Women Who Think Too Much: How to Break Free of Overthinking and Reclaim Your Life* (2004), stating that women are a little bit more likely to overthink than men, but not by that large of a margin: women 57% and men 43%. Nolen-Hoeksema also reports that younger adults are more susceptible than older ones, with 73% of 25–35 year olds succumbing to the habit, 52% of 45–55 year olds, and just 20% of those aged 65–75. Though the numbers differ, it's apparent that too many people think too much. This is a dangerous trend because rumination leads nowhere good. It often results in depression, anxiety, and even alcoholism.

If you're not careful, overthinking can be chronic, but it's not incurable. With a bit of humor and a lot of insight—and with a little humility and loads of encouragement—you can pull yourself free from its grip and turn it into something you can monitor, manage, and manipulate if not entirely eliminate.

Stop Your Stinking Overthinking: Strategies for Quieting the Busy Mind, Letting Go, and Staying Present will equip you with tools to manage and reduce overthinking and help you achieve a healthier state of mind and a more present life. In these pages, you will discover

- tools and techniques to regulate your nervous system.

- strategies to retrain your mind to new and empowering habits.

- tips to manage and reduce overthinking and enhance your overall well-being.

- personal anecdotes and real-life examples that illustrate the negative effects of overthinking.

- ways to put a stop to your stinking overthinking.

You are not doomed to overthink for eternity—or even for the duration of your existence on this planet. But you are destined to free yourself from this burden of excessive thoughts and to stop letting rumination steal your joy in the *now*.

I didn't prove Stevie Nicks wrong; I didn't come to any conclusion at all. *Does* thunder only happen when it's raining? I may never know, no matter how much I crank the gears in my brain, and they're tempted to start spinning again...

Instead of getting back on that rollercoaster, let's buckle up, get ready to laugh at the brain's most ridiculous antics, and learn practical steps to stop that stinking overthinking!

Chapter 1:

Understanding

Overthinking

Amit Ray, an Indian author and philosopher, taught, "Overthinking is not a disease; it is due to the underuse of your creative power" (Ray, n.d.). Wait a minute! Dostoyevsky said it *is* a disease, so is it or isn't it? Yes. No. Both!

Overthinking is not a psychological disorder, nor is it a physiological ailment. However, if allowed to dominate your mind, it can result in mental health conditions like anxiety and depression, which, *if allowed to dominate your mind*, can lead to physical maladies like heart conditions, diabetes, and hypertension—in other words, disease.

When you overthink, you're certainly utilizing your imagination, being innovative, and creatively attempting to think yourself out of the box your rumination has put you in. When you overthink, you trick yourself into believing the solution is just one idea away. But when you get there, that concept isn't right either; the real answer is just one *more* idea away. So the cycle rolls on and on, and you get stuck in this pattern until Ray's notion proves true: An underuse of your creative power keeps you locked in the box.

Why Do We Overthink?

Overthinking occurs when you excessively analyze situations or potential outcomes. However, since you don't arrive at a solution, you often end up distressed by your indecision. Sometimes, an event or thought can trigger this loop of analysis and make you spiral out of control. For instance, if someone sends a short text message, you might spend hours guessing what it means. *Did they mean to be rude? Are they upset?* This process of worrying can consume your mind and distract you from more important tasks.

Why do we overthink in the first place? Oftentimes, it's due to one of these issues:

- **Your brain has no off switch:** You keep replaying the events or conversations you're worried about, thinking of every "if only" and "what if" and contemplating different scenarios. When you go to bed, those thoughts may still be swirling. You glance at the clock and realize several hours have passed—you're still awake, and then you dread the next day at the office because you're sure to be exhausted from not sleeping, and you think about how that's sure not gonna help you resolve that awkward situation with the boss—you're reminded of what you said to your boss the day before, and then you're back to the beginning again... Sigh. Normal thoughts can sometimes process for a while, but you eventually come to a conclusion—you hit the off switch—but overthinking only has a snooze button. It's like how time ticks to eternity; you might prolong the start of your day, but eventually, it resumes.

- **You're indecisive:** Have you convinced yourself that the longer you think about something and the more effort you put into it, the more angles you will cover and the more perspectives you'll consider? It would be okay if you stopped right there and accepted a decision, but what happens instead is that you obsess and overanalyze until all those options become barriers. Research suggests that extended contemplation delays decision-making, and that it's not until you have a distraction from that thought process that your mind can actually assess the information and come to a conclusion (Strick et al., 2010).

- **You second-guess every decision:** Overthinking often begins innocently enough with the good intention to solve a problem or fix something that went wrong. It might even be something fun, like where to plan a vacation. Rumination's not picky. It'll even bring up that day in middle school when you and your best friend argued over who would wear the one and only tiara to the dance, and you fought over it until it broke, and now you're trying to figure out what you could have done differently. But I digress. You're actually spinning your wheels on whether you should go to the beach or the mountains. Should you take the kids or leave them with Grandma and Grandpa while you and your special other have a little getaway? You could make great family memories at the beach, learning to surf, collecting shells, and hunting ghost crabs, but your son's not a strong swimmer, and your daughter hates the sand, so maybe you should stay in a cabin by the lake. You can make great memories with your spouse there, cuddling by the fire, sipping coffee on the deck as the sun rises over the trees, and rowing out on the water to catch some fish... but you are terrified of snakes, which are definitely in wooded areas, and your partner couldn't catch a fish to save their life, and... No decision is *right*.

- **You are not focused on solutions:** You might begin with a problem that needs a solution, but once your mental wheels start spinning, you quickly end up far off the beaten path, trying to figure out what it was you were trying to figure out in the first place. Overthinking means dwelling on the problem, not focusing on a solution. Remember the thunderstorm I mentioned in the introduction? I was *dwelling on the problem* of lightning, thunder, and heavy rain.

I was not considering any options to lessen my dog's fear (aside from holding him), doing anything to quiet the noise, or providing him with a comfort blanket or toy. Those things would have been *solutions*. If my mind had tracked that course, my time would have been productive. As it was, I didn't achieve anything; I just humored my imagination.

- **You replay thoughts or rehash conversations:** Raise your hand if this is you! (Me, me, me!) I can't count the times I've done this after a disagreement or an embarrassing moment. The scene runs through my mind over and over, and each time, my face flushes red again. *I said what? I should have said [fill in the blank]! Next time, I'll say it [this way], and I won't sound so dumb/silly/foolish.* Or I'll think of the perfect comeback at like 3 a.m., when it's way too late to text that person what I meant to say, and way too much time has passed since I said that, and if I bring it back up now, I'll just be embarrassed all over again.

- **You struggle with stressful situations:** Stressful situations like job interviews, arguments with friends, or even changes in routine can all trigger overthinking. Perfectionism, fear of failure, and certain other psychological patterns you rely on exacerbate overthinking. A perfectionist might replay every detail of a presentation—similar to what I mentioned in the previous section—fearing they did not do it perfectly or realizing things they could have said to make the presentation more effective. When you overthink, you become consumed by that one thing to the detriment of everything else. What if you are rehashing that presentation—which probably was a success—when you should be moving forward with putting that proposal into action? You waste your time and mental energy on something that's in the past and cannot be changed, and you fall behind in the progress you should be making.

Did you find yourself in any of those examples? If you're like me, you identified with more than one, and that's normal. We all tend to overthink sometimes; it's only problematic when it interferes with your daily life. Whether at work or home, recognizing this habit and being aware of the triggers are essential steps toward overcoming overthinking. Putting a stop to overthinking frees you to be more productive in all areas of life. Let's talk more about this and get a better understanding of what we're dealing with.

Emotional Reasoning and Its Impact

Emotions are quick and often imprecise responses to situations. In the 1970s, American psychologist Paul Eckman identified six key emotions all humans experience: happiness, sadness, disgust, fear, anger, and surprise. Psychologist Robert Plutchik later arranged those emotions in pairs opposite each other, similar to a color wheel. This "wheel of emotions" has since been further developed to place many more complex emotions—such as embarrassment, shame, or pride—in various areas of overlap (Cherry, 2024).

Emotions influence the way you engage with people and affect how you live your life. Some emotions alert you to danger; others comfort you with feelings of security. All, however, have the potential to lead to poor decision-making if you allow them to dominate your reasoning process. For example, if you feel sad, you might fixate on other sad things and fall into a spiral of negativity.

This is why emotional reasoning (ER) is intertwined with overthinking. ER distorts your perceptions. When you engage in emotional reasoning, you believe something is true just because you *feel* it to be true. For instance, you may feel angry that a friend canceled plans because you think this means they don't value your friendship. You're using emotions as evidence instead of relying on logic or observable facts.

If unchecked, this behavior can ruin relationships and create problems that aren't really there. Overreliance on emotions can worsen anxiety and lead you to make decisions without support for your conclusion.

To better manage emotions, you need to distinguish between your emotional mind—a more reactive and impulsive state—and your rational mind, which is logical but can seem cold. A balanced approach, according to Emma McAdam of Therapy in a Nutshell (2024), is to cultivate what is called the wise mind. The wise mind acknowledges emotions while also considering logic and reason.

One effective way to recognize emotional reasoning is through cognitive behavioral therapy (CBT) techniques, which encourage you to challenge your thoughts systematically. For example, instead of letting sadness dictate your belief about your friendship, examine the situation logically. Your friend probably had a valid reason to cancel that had nothing at all to do with you. We'll discuss CBT further in a later chapter. For now, let's focus on some things you can do to jumpstart your overthinking recovery.

Strategies to Combat Overthinking

One practical method to combat overthinking is to slow down your reactions. There's plenty of time between a stimulus and your response to take a thoughtful pause. Take that moment to breathe, count, or simply reflect on the situation so you don't make a rash decision.

Predicting emotional triggers can also be incredibly helpful. For instance, there's a family gathering coming up, and you don't get along with your sister-in-law. Just the thought of being in the same room with her sends your mind into a loop, overthinking, rethinking, and emotionally thinking about that thing she said last Christmas that insulted your mother, sent your niece running for cover, and drove a wedge between you and your brother. As the scene starts to play in your head, and the reels whip through your brain like an old drive-in filmstrip, you fall down, down, down into the pit of anger and hostility, contemplating all the things you're going to say to her the moment you see her, *overthinking, rethinking, and emotionally thinking* through them again and again until you're exhausted. Your sister-in-law is a trigger. Be aware of that and plan accordingly. You might ask your spouse to give you a subtle signal if they notice you're getting frustrated, and it will remind you to step back and calm down before returning to the conversation.

In some situations, you can take the opposite action of what your emotions tell you to do. If the emotional response is urging you to shout in anger, speak softly instead. If you feel the urge to overthink, the opposite—underthinking—probably wouldn't be very helpful either. In this case, don't ruminate—proactivate! Okay, I made up that word, but what you need to do is proactively consider the subject. Don't just spin your wheels; give purpose to your thoughts.

Another practical approach is to write down how to handle such situations better next time. This helps to solidify your understanding of your emotional responses and creates a strategic plan for future instances.

Understanding Intrusive and Automatic Thought Patterns

Intrusive thoughts are unwanted mental images or ideas that come into your mind without warning and cause distress. Some can be disturbing, like sudden thoughts of violence or inappropriate situations, and are commonly associated with anxiety, obsessive-compulsive disorder (OCD), and post-traumatic stress disorder (PTSD). People dealing with these issues might experience intrusive thoughts more frequently because of their predisposition and end up in a cycle of worry that impacts their daily lives.

Automatic thought patterns differ from intrusive ones in that they are not interrupters. They are the unconscious beliefs you hold about yourself and the world around you. For example, if you got turned down for a job promotion, you might unconsciously believe you are unworthy of success. Such assumptions can influence how you respond to situations and shape your perceptions and emotions, even when there is no real evidence to support them.

Shift Your Perspective

Cognitive fusion occurs when you become entangled with your thoughts and lose sight of the present moment. It can be detrimental and lead to increased stress and anxiety. To counteract the impact of intrusive and automatic thoughts, you need to change the way you view them. Instead of letting thoughts control you, learn to observe and analyze them. Below are some ways to achieve this goal:

- **Cognitive defusion:** In contrast to cognitive fusion, cognitive defusion involves detaching yourself from your thoughts and emotions rather than letting them dictate your actions. To practice cognitive defusion, examine your thoughts as if they are merely passing words in a stream. Instead of engaging with negative thoughts or trying to suppress them, acknowledge their existence and choose whether to focus on them or let them go. This approach helps reduce the burden of negative thinking and fosters psychological flexibility.

- **Acceptance and commitment therapy (ACT):** Cognitive defusion is often utilized in combination with ACT to help you accept your thoughts and feelings while committing to actions that align with your values. As you focus on what truly matters to you, you begin to let go of the power that intrusive and automatic thoughts hold over you. Identifying core values and engaging in activities that reflect these values can bring more meaning to your life and diminish the grip of negative thoughts.

- **Mindfulness:** Set aside a few minutes each day to practice mindfulness, which can help train you to acknowledge intrusive thoughts without letting them control you. Keep a thought journal and review it regularly to identify thought patterns and become more aware of your thought processes. Build a supportive network around you and seek professional guidance.

Productive Reflection vs. Destructive Overthinking

I mentioned previously that many people mistakenly believe that overthinking is beneficial, that the more they analyze a subject, the more perspectives they'll get on it, and the better able they'll be to make an informed decision. That would be considered *productive* thinking, which would be fine; however, overthinking just stirs the concoction of possibilities into a big pot of murky mess!

Personal reflection—an act of productive thinking—involves taking the time to thoughtfully consider and analyze your thoughts, experiences, and actions. It's a process of self-examination and introspection that helps you gain insight into your emotions, motivations, and values. Through personal reflection, you can better understand yourself, improve self-awareness, and make positive changes in your life. It's a self-assessment from which you arrive at an actionable conclusion.

Destructive overthinking refers to the excessive and harmful habit of constantly dwelling on negative thoughts and scenarios—when you focus on the downside of a situation instead of the positive. It can lead to feelings of pessimism, hopelessness, anxiety, and stress and make it difficult to make decisions or take action. This type of overthinking can be detrimental to your mental and emotional well-being and may hinder your ability to function effectively.

Catastrophizing is a form of destructive overthinking that refers to the tendency to perceive a situation as considerably worse than it actually is. It's when you magnify the importance of negative events, expect the worst imaginable outcome, and live as if that's the reality of the moment. Naturally, when you're in this state of cognitive distortion, your anxiety skyrockets, and your distress plummets.

Let's say you were in a tizzy this morning because you overslept—slammed that snooze button five times, to be honest—and put yourself in a crazed rush to get dressed, out the door, and in the office within 45 minutes. You plop down at your desk and wonder *Did I turn off the coffee maker?* You glance at the insulated mug in your hand and remember emptying the pot into it. *If the burner's still on, there's nothing in the carafe to warm. It'll just keep heating the glass, but there's nothing in it! And I left the dish towel right there on the counter beside it. If the machine keeps running, the glass will overheat, it will explode, and the towel will catch on fire! That will spread to the window curtain, and the walls, and the cabinets. My whole house is going to burn down before lunch!* You can't call the neighbors to check. The ones you do know are at work now, and no one has a key to your house anyway. All morning, you worry away. *Surely, the fire department would call if my home caught fire, right? But how would they know how to reach me?* The report you just handed your boss was interspersed with reminders to double-check things and buy a fire extinguisher, and somehow, "Give my neighbor Cindy a key to my house" was worked into the final paragraph. It's noon when he knocks on your office door with a really puzzled look on his face, but no sound comes from his mouth because he's whiplashed by your mad dash outside to your car. He's left there blinking in confusion as you race home—*gotta beat the firetruck there!*

Was that personal reflection, looking back on your peaceful morning to ponder the delicious coffee you brought to work with you? No. It was down and dirty, destructive, catastrophizing! You didn't just wonder; you worried, feared, and then convinced yourself of the most disastrous possibility. The thoughts going through your mind were not helpful in any way. They did not give you new perspectives or help you reach a logical conclusion. Instead, they set your anxiety off like fireworks and compromised the quality of your work.

Take heart! There are several ways to challenge negative thinking. Here are some tips that may help:

- **Seek professional help:** Consulting a mental health professional such as a therapist or counselor can provide you with the necessary support and guidance. They can help you understand your emotions, identify triggers, and develop coping mechanisms.

- **Build a support system:** Reach out to friends and family members for support. Talking about your feelings and experiences with trusted individuals can provide emotional relief and help you feel less isolated.

- **Practice self-care:** Engage in activities that promote self-care and relaxation, such as exercise, bubble baths, or hobbies that you enjoy.

- **Cognitive restructuring:** This is a therapeutic process that involves identifying and challenging negative thought patterns and replacing them with more constructive, rational beliefs that improve mental well-being and enhance decision-making skills.

- **Mindfulness techniques:** Meditation and deep breathing, can help bring awareness to negative thought patterns, restore you to an accurate sense of the present moment, and promote a more positive mindset.

- **Establish a routine:** Create and stick to a daily routine to add structure and stability to your daily life. Prioritize healthy habits, such as regular sleep patterns, balanced nutrition, and staying physically active.

- **Challenge negative thoughts:** Cognitive-behavioral therapy techniques can help you challenge distorted and negative thinking patterns that contribute to depression and anxiety. Learning to reframe your thoughts in a more positive and realistic manner can make a significant difference.

- **Set realistic goals:** Break large tasks into smaller, achievable goals. Reaching small goals can build a sense of accomplishment, boost your confidence, and contribute to a more positive outlook.

- **Limit stress:** Identify sources of stress in your life and develop strategies to manage or minimize them. You could set boundaries, delegate tasks, or practice relaxation techniques.

Be patient and compassionate with yourself as you work through these strategies.

Oh, Stop It!

Wouldn't it be nice if you could just tell your mental gears to quit spinning? While stopping your stinking overthinking might not be quite that simple to stifle, effective management of those tendencies comes down to "engaging in daily actions that will train you not to overreact and remain in control from the inside out." To accomplish this retraining, try the following tips (Mara, 2024):

- Identify your triggers.

- Recognize when you start to overthink.

- Rein in those thoughts and put them to work finding a solution; don't just let them spin.

- Understand that the problem is not the problem, but overthinking is.

- Consider if the thing you're pondering will still be worth considering in a week. If not, let it drop.

- Allow yourself to stop at "good enough" and don't pursue the perfect answer.

Author and well-being coach Shira Gura (n.d.) promotes an "unSTUCK" method:

- **S**top: Pause to separate your thoughts from the emotional reaction that has arisen to them.

- **T**ell: If strong emotions are attached to your thoughts, get them out in the open and acknowledge them.

- **U**ncover: Investigate your thoughts and give validity to truthful ones.

- **C**onsider: Replace illegitimate thoughts with truthful ones.

- **K**indness: Be kind to yourself! Don't beat yourself up for your struggles; allow yourself to feel and to heal.

Keep these suggestions in mind as we move ahead. In the next chapter, we'll explore the mind-body connection and get a better understanding of how overthinking impacts your overall well-being. We'll also discuss strategies to combat mental stress and learn about grounding techniques.

Chapter 2:

Understanding Your Mind-Body Connection

In the previous chapter, we talked a lot about how overthinking can increase stress and how that heightened anxiety can lead to physical discomforts, ailments, and diseases, like heart conditions and diabetes. In this chapter, we're going to flip that flop and consider how your body's *physical* condition can impact your *mental* state.

The terms "mental health" and "emotional health" both refer to the function of your mind and are often used interchangeably. However, the two have some important differences:

- **Mental health** refers to how we think, solve problems, and make decisions. It is the more physical aspect of the mind and involves brain processes, mental disorders (like chemical imbalances), and behavior and personality changes.

- **Emotional health** has to do with feelings and how we experience and manage them. It deals with insecurities and fears as well as joy and satisfaction and also moderates social skills and self-regulation.

Both aspects, however, are interrelated when it comes to the mind-body connection.

A recent study from the Washington University School of Medicine (2023) revealed that the mind and body affect each other in physiological and not just abstract ways. Researchers claim their findings confirm a literal link within the brain's physical structure between these two components of the human being that were thought to operate separately. They state, "Parts of the brain area that control movement are plugged into networks involved in thinking and planning, and in control of involuntary bodily functions such as blood pressure and heartbeat." We tend to think that thoughts and feelings are distinct from bodily functions and movements, but this demonstrates that the two parts (mind and body) work together, not independently.

In the pages that follow, we will focus on the body-mind connection, learn about how some of your negative and strong emotions can be stored deep down in your body, and understand how that physical emotional storage affects not only your mental well-being but also your physical health.

Mind-Body Connection: How Emotions Affect Health

The study mentioned above has helped researchers understand *why* anxiety has accompanying physical symptoms, *why* vagus nerve stimulation relieves depression, and *why* regular exercise can lead to a more positive outlook. Though such correlations have long been known, science is just now starting to discover the links that connect these networks. It's enabled them to explain how the mind and body have a back-and-forth communication track such that the one affects the other and the other affects the one.

This is why meditation, yoga, and deep breathing calm the body *and* the mind, and it is why high anxiety stresses the body *and* the mind. As Professor Evan Gordon of the Mallinckrodt Institute of Radiology explains (as cited in Washington University School of Medicine, 2023):

> We've found the place where the highly active, goal-oriented "go, go, go" part of your mind connects to the parts of the brain that control breathing and heart rate. If you calm one down, it absolutely should have feedback effects on the other (para. 4).

While it's not new information, this revelation provides a tangible approach to something previously considered only in philosophical—and in more recent centuries—psychological circles.

The ancient Greek physician Hippocrates and those who studied under him are thought to be among the first people in recorded history to attempt to understand emotions. In their work, they pulled from ancient science and philosophy as they explored the endocrine, nervous, and immune systems, as well as structural parts of the body, in search of the inner workings and their connection to disorders and diseases.

Hippocrates and his followers developed "the theory of the four humors," which assessed a person's health based on the "humors" of blood, phlegm, black bile, and yellow bile. They concluded that when those four were in balance, a person was in good health, but if any was unbalanced, disease prevailed. Their prognosis aimed to restore the balance by improving the patient's diet, increasing their amount of physical activity, and managing the body's excretions of urine, feces, blood, and perspiration.

Greek physician Galen, who lived about 500 years after Hippocrates, based his practice on Hippocrates' humoral factors but expanded his diagnostic skill to include monitoring the pulse. In this case, he was often able to discern between organic ailments and those traced to the emotions.

Twelfth century physician, Moses Maimonides, took Galen's ideas a step further, attributing "passions of the psyche" to "changes in the body that are great, evident, and manifest to all," and he advised they be kept in balance as the topmost priority. Later scholars suggested that the imagination also contributed to nonphysical ailments by inciting the emotions, which then disrupted the body's physical condition. "Vivid ideas" were even thought to cause "monstrous births," a persistent concern that lasted well into the 19th century (Frontiers of the Mind, 2023).

A shift occurred in the 18th century, when they study of anatomy became the foundation of pathology. Physicians at this time concluded that disease resulted from what they called "lesions," or parts of the body that were susceptible to ailment, rather than emotional or humoral imbalances. As the 19th century rolled around, inventions like the stethoscope led to improved patient diagnostics and furthered the promotion of anatomical conditions as the primary explanation for disease, drifting away from mental or emotional influence.

At about the same time, study of the nervous system was developing and quickly became a dumping ground for things that couldn't be explained away by faulty anatomy. Hysteria and insanity were said to result from "a considerable and unusual excess in the excitement of the brain" or "violent emotions or passions of the mind," and many conditions, like epilepsy, were even considered to be imaginary complaints of people who were seeking attention (Frontiers of the Mind, 2023).

Throughout the 20th century, advancements in medical equipment allowed audio and visual glimpses inside the body and the study of tissues and cells at microscopic levels. This, combined with the growth of the psychology field, which began in the late 1800s with such pioneers as Sigmund Freud and Joseph Breuer, further distanced the notion of psychological influence over health and disease and separated the two areas of science.

The wheel seems to be turning once more toward acceptance of the mind and body connection, and it has influenced the development of integrative medicine, a field of medical science that bases diagnosis and treatment on the condition of the whole person, taking into account both mental and physiological states.

Strategies to Use Physical Wellness to Combat Mental Stress

Many of those early theorizations from Hippocrates, Galen, and others were on the right track. They understood that there was a mind-body correlation, but they could not seem to find concrete evidence. Hence, their theories eventually lost momentum in favor of tangible scientific "proof." Today, we have the benefit of learning from both camps—emotional study and anatomy—and can get a more complete picture of how the mind and body philosophically *and* physiologically work together to achieve overall health and wellness.

Director of the U.S. Office of Disease Prevention and Health Promotion, Dr. Paul Reed (2021), notes the sort of catch-22 loop. Ill physical health yields ill mental health; conversely, optimal physical health yields optimal mental health. Reed says, "What's good for the body is often good for the mind," and recommends the following tips to keep both physical and mental health in tip-top order:

- **Get moving!** Moderate to vigorous physical activity wards off all sorts of illnesses and ailments and improves your cognitive functions. Exercise has specifically been shown to increase the amount of norepinephrine, a neurotransmitter that helps the brain deal with stress. In fact, 50% of the brain's norepinephrine supply is located in an area involving emotional responses (*Working Out Boosts Brain Health*, 2020). The U.S. Department of Health and Human Services (2018) promotes the following physical activity guidelines for adults:

    ○ Move more; sit less. You will benefit from any movement that is moderate to vigorous.

    ○ Do moderate to vigorous muscle-strengthening activity at least two days a week.

    ○ Get 150–300 minutes of moderate or 75–150 minutes of vigorous aerobic activity throughout the course of each week. Get more benefits from additional cardio work.

- **Have a mental health screening.** Request this from your healthcare provider regularly as a preventative measure and to moderate existing conditions. If necessary, seek therapeutic benefit from professional help.

- **Take in ample nutrition.** Fuel your body well to give it the healthy sustenance it needs. Include foods that boost your brain power, too, for improved overall well-being.

While physical activity cannot substitute for mental health treatments, it can contribute to sustained mind *and* body wellness. This statement concisely sums up the mind-body connection and the importance of keeping both parts of your being functioning well (*Working Out Boosts Brain Health*, 2020):

> The cardiovascular system communicates with the renal system, which communicates with the muscular system. And all of these are controlled by the central and sympathetic nervous systems, which also must communicate with each other. This workout of the body's communication system may be the true value of exercise; the more sedentary we get, the less efficient our bodies are in responding to stress (para. 7).

It kind of reminds me of the old "bones" song to teach children the skeletal system. You know, "The head bone's connected to the neck bones. The neck bones' are connected to the backbone. The backbone's connected to the hip bone..." Maybe we could borrow the tune but change the words to, "The cardiovascular system's connected to the renal system. The renal system is connected to the muscular system. And they're all controlled by the nervous system..." But I don't think it has the same catchy ring.

Where Deep-Seated Emotions Are Stored in the Body

Emotions can be uncomfortable, especially the negative ones; although, pleasant experiences can be overwhelming too. When you feel something too much—if it's too scary to confront, if it hurts too much, if you fear the trauma will happen again, if you worry the repercussions will be too severe, if you've overthought too much and it now feels catastrophic— you may try to push those emotions deep down inside to a hidden place where they're no longer in your face. Instead of tackling those feelings head-on, you bottle them up. The problem is that whenever you avoid processing your emotions, you keep yourself in perpetual inner conflict.

According to Sean Grover of *Psychology Today* (2018), repression feeds fear and triggers psychosomatic symptoms. He describes 10 areas of the body in which these stuffed-away emotions are stored. You might experience these symptoms individually, but they can also occur in combination, depending on your emotional state:

- **Hurt:** A broken heart is not just a thing of fairy tales and sappy movies. The heart is your natural center of love, devotion, and deep-seated sentiment. When someone hurts you, and you don't fully process it all the way through to a place of healing, you may feel tightness in your chest and, yes, pain in your heart.

- **Anxiety:** Approximately 40 million American adults are affected by anxiety disorders each year. That's more than 19% of the population! I'll admit I'm one of those 40 million (*Anxiety Disorder—Facts & Statistics*, 2022). Though I have a magic power of being super calm in the middle of crises, I don't handle stress very well in general. Anxious feelings often manifest in breathing difficulty—in various forms like shortness of breath, shallow breath, or rapid breath—and are sometimes accompanied by lightheadedness and potential incidents of passing out.

- **Loss of self-identity:** When you feel like your life is in flux, when major changes have occurred and turned life upside down, and you no longer identify the you that you thought you were—even if it's a good experience, like building your personal growth—you'll likely experience sleep disturbances like insomnia, frequent wakings, or trouble getting back to sleep once you are awake.

- **Fear:** This is a very common effect. It definitely happens to me! When you are afraid, your stomach may cramp or roil, and you may feel the need to purge. Gut complaints are closely linked to conflict and being afraid of the outcome (or a fear of not knowing what will happen next). It can be fear of physically dangerous things or situations or personal confrontations and disagreements.

- **Anger:** "Oh, my aching back!" If you haven't said it yourself, you've likely heard it on TV during a comedic moment when one character is frustrated with another. In reality, lower back pain is not a laughing matter, so try to work through and resolve frustration whenever you encounter it.

- **Loss of control:** If you are strong-willed, if you are a control freak, or if you feel like your plans have all gone wrong, you could develop a headache. Control tendencies can make a situation worse, which, in turn, can make you feel worse and develop migraines or some of the other symptoms in this list, like back pain, neck tension, or anxiety.

- **Trauma:** Trauma can be a physical incident in which you were injured, threatened, or experienced a severe loss, but it can also occur from anything that impacts you intensely on an emotional level. If these feelings are not worked through early on, you risk becoming numb to your feelings so that you don't feel that critical harm again. You deaden your feelings to eliminate vulnerability.

- **Oppression:** You have the right to be heard! But perhaps, instead, you've been stifled. Persistent silencing creates an inner conflict of wanting to speak up but fearing either harsh consequences or having your words land on deaf ears. The resulting tension can constrict the muscles in your throat and make your voice hoarse or raspy.

- **Resentment:** When you resent someone, you give them power over you—in your head. You don't hurt them at all, but you do continue to wear yourself down. As an overthinker, you probably know this already! Reliving conflicts, confrontations, arguments, and uncomfortable or frustrating situations is exhausting, isn't it? Fatigue results when you're busy hashing out all that blame and anger inside your mind.

- **Burden:** Shouldering too much responsibility— even if you've unnecessarily placed it upon yourself—can really be a pain in the neck. When you feel overburdened, your neck, shoulders, and upper back can tighten up with a lot of tension and lead to headaches, jaw displacement, and spinal shifts, increasing the discomfort you already feel in your upper body.

Not all ailments are psychosomatic, of course, but because the mind and body are connected by emotion and physiology, you may literally feel your feelings.

Learning to Deal With Strong and Overwhelming Emotions

Doctors often advise their patients to reduce the stress in their lives, but is it really possible to reduce stress? I'm not so sure! What you can do, however, is deal with it.

You might be in the middle of a stressful situation, and it may come to a resolution. However, does that mean the stress is gone? Not necessarily. Something could be worked out but still be difficult, especially if things didn't go your way. What you really need to do—and the only way to minimize the effects of stress on your life—is to learn how to *manage* stress.

Below are some strategies to use your body to calm your mind and progress toward getting your overthinking under control:

- Allow your emotions to brew, but limit the time you dedicate to them to no more than an hour a day. As you grow accustomed to scheduling contemplation (or overthink) time, shorten it in increments until you give those thoughts only five minutes a day.

- Ground yourself with techniques like sensory awareness exercises. The 5-4-3-2-1 exercise is my personal go-to! It's simple and very enjoyable, and it can be done anywhere at any time. Situate yourself in a quiet place where you won't be disturbed. Then, run—actually, no, walk slowly—through each of your 5 senses, listing 5, 4, 3, 2, or 1 of the things you sense around you. For example, start with 5 things you can hear, then 4 things you can see, 3 things you can touch, 2 things you can smell, and 1 thing you can taste. Go through them again, but change up the senses and try 5 things you can smell, 4 things you can touch, and so on.

- Practice breathing exercises. Qigong is a healing art that was established in ancient China and involves controlled breathing and movement as well as meditation. Allison Lim of the Traditional Chinese Medicine World Foundation (2022) explains that the practice targets specific parts of the body and the stressors that are affecting them. For example, heart qi balances peace and harmony throughout the body, while liver qi manages anxiety and stress, and lung qi processes grief. If you're not familiar with qigong, the 4-7-8 breathing technique is a good one to get you started. Again, find a quiet place and eliminate interruptions. Sit in a comfortable chair and keep your back straight with your feet flat on the floor. Inhale deeply for a count of 4 seconds; hold that breath for a count of 7 seconds; then slowly release it for a count of 8 seconds.

- Do yoga. Yoga is a wonderful practice to relax both the mind and the body—and those connectors that keep both aspects bumping off each other. Traditional yoga can be done at beginner, intermediate, and advanced levels to suit your abilities, and chair yoga has become a popular method for seniors or those with mobility or other health issues that prevent them from performing the full range of movements.

- Walk with intention in a mindful manner. Mindfulness—which we'll discuss in depth in the next chapter—is the practice of allowing yourself to embrace your feelings in a nonjudgmental way that pulls your focus off your troubles and centers it in the present moment. There are many ways to practice mindfulness, but sensory walking is a great way to use your body to relieve your mind. You walk every day, so it's not a sport or a skill you need to learn. Just extend it to lengthier efforts, like doing a lap or two around your neighborhood, and focus on the sensations you encounter on the journey. *Hear* the bird songs, *feel* the sun's warmth on your cheeks, and *breathe in* the fresh, clean air. What other sounds do you hear? What scents blow in the breeze? Did you feel the flutter of the butterfly that brushed your arm? Did you see that cat scamper under the fence?

Other ways to relax your nervous system and pacify your mind include doing light exercise, getting an emotional support pet or engaging more with the pet you have, replacing negative thoughts with positive ones, establishing and enforcing boundaries, tending to self-care, and picking up a hobby.

Healthy coping skills like the ones we've discussed here help you calm your mind and body from the effects of stress without repressing your feelings or avoiding the issues. When you're ready, you'll be more able to think with purpose, arrive at actionable conclusions, stop ruminating, and quit running your mind and body ragged.

Chapter 3:

Mastering Mindfulness

Stress is your body's way of telling you it can't handle what you've got going on. You can't really avoid it. Even if you were a hermit, you might still worry about your provisions, your health, or what would happen if some developer bulldozed your location to build the next megamall.

Your body is designed to react to stress. It's meant to keep you safe from harm. Stress responses can be positive or negative, but both help your body adjust to new experiences. If you're that hermit gathering firewood in the forest, and you turn around and greet a grizzly face-to-face, stress will be a good thing because it will trigger your fight-or-flight response and jumpstart your body to do what it needs to survive. If, however, you get stuck in lengthy overthinking sessions every day wondering what it would be like to live alone in the woods... *Would I prefer a cabin or an earthen structure? Would I have to cook everything over an open fire? Can a hermit have modern amenities? I mean, they're not necessarily going off-grid. They just want to get away from people. Would online orders still get delivered? What about pizza? Do they even have phone service or the internet? What if I were a hermit, and I came face-to-face with a grizzly while gathering firewood? What do you do with grizzlies, run away? No, I think you play dead. No problem, I'd probably pass out anyway. But then, it might think, "Yum!*

*Fresh meat!" and have a go at me. And being a hermit, no one's around to hear me holler for help. Forget what happens when a tree falls in a forest; if you scream during a bear attack and no one's around to hear it, do you make a sound? ...*you'd find yourself stuck in critical fight-or-flight tension with nothing to actually fight or flee from.

You would've wound yourself up for no reason at all. That kind of stress is harmful. It increases your heart rate, makes you breathe rapidly, and releases cortisol, which, since it doesn't have a real job to do—like boost your metabolism and ready you to throw punches or run like lightning—just builds up in your body. Persistent cortisol release brought on by the stress you place yourself under when you ruminate and obsess over your stressors can greatly increase your risk of developing heart disease, obesity, anxiety, lung issues, and other physical ailments.

Aside from excessive contemplation, numerous other life factors contribute to high levels of stress. Everyday worries like work duties, family responsibilities, paying bills, and even going on vacation—yes, it's true—can result in any or all of the three types of stress:

- **Acute:** This is short-term, positive, or negative stress that comes and goes, like angst before a job interview or the trill of a roller coaster's fist drop.

- **Episodic:** This is recurring acute stress that you encounter regularly so that you don't have time to recover from one incident before being plunged into the next. First responders often experience this.

- **Chronic:** This is prolonged stress that lasts for weeks or months. You might feel this during a health crisis or during a difficult relationship.

You might have an acute stress response if you occasionally overthink, episodic if you do it a few times a week, and chronic if you ruminate daily, especially multiple times a day or for long periods at a time. And you might start to notice some of those psychosomatic symptoms we discussed in the previous chapter. Reliving harsh confrontations may keep hurting your heart, rehashing fretful what-ifs might keep your stomach tied in knots, and constantly worrying over responsibilities can keep your shoulders hunched up to your ears.

What can you do to relieve all this stress and reduce its effects? In Chapter 2, we gave you some strategies for putting your body to work to restore peace of mind, and we touched on mindfulness practices as one of those techniques. Mindfulness offers so many options and provides so many benefits that we are devoting this entire chapter to it.

Buddhist monk Thich Nhat Hanh (n.d.) wisely observed, "With mindfulness, you can establish yourself in the present in order to touch the wonders of life that are available in that moment." So let's learn what mindfulness is, dispel myths to discern what it's not, discover how it differs from meditation, and learn how to start practicing this technique.

What Is Mindfulness?

Did you know that your brain is plastic? It's funny to apply that term to such a complex organ, but it comes straight from the Latin *plasticus* (minus the suffix), meaning "of molding," and the Greek *plastikos*, meaning "to mold or form" (M-W, n.d.). In essence, your brain can be shaped and changed—it actually is every day by the act of neuroplasticity. By adding the Greek *neura* or *neuron* to the beginning, we specify that we're talking about "nerves," as Galen interpreted it from the original meaning of "sinew" or "string" (Online Etymology Dictionary, n.d.).

Neuroplasticity

Dr. Richard Davidson, a psychologist, researcher, and professor at the University of Wisconsin-Madison, is known for his studies on the effects of meditation on neurological conditions, specifically in regard to the brain's ability to morph throughout the course of life (neuroplasticity, if you weren't paying attention, wink-wink). Traditionally, Western science has considered the brain static, but Davidson challenged that theory when he hotwired some monks' brains.

Davidson chose to examine Tibetan Buddhist monks because they are "masters of the art of dispassionately observing the inner workings of their own minds," and so determined they, of all people, would be the best subjects for his inquiry. His study linked states of consciousness to the central nervous system's electrical activity and revealed that the strong neural activity associated with meditation takes place in the left prefrontal cortex and amygdala (Weil, 2006).

What Davidson discovered was that the long-term practice of meditation altered not only the function of the monks' brains but their structure as well, including the growth of new neurons and the establishment of new connections within the brain's circuitry. Davidson and his team were able to observe these changes, the impact in the prefrontal cortex brought on by visual stimulation, and circuitry changes in amplitude and frequency with the use of functional magnetic resonance imaging (fMRI), quantitative electrophysiology, and positron emission topography—basically high tech machines that can see into your mind (Davidson & Lutz, 2008).

Davidson's studies led the way for further research, such as that more recently conducted by Dr. Lisa Feldman Barrett, a psychology professor at Northwestern University. Feldman Barrett's studies challenge the notion that the brain has dedicated circuits for the fight-or-flight response. Basing her conclusions on much stronger fMRIs than what are standardly used (seven-tesla magnification as opposed to three-tesla), which can see deeper into small, localized regions of the brain—the periaqueductal gray

(PAG), in particular—her team has been able to observe the amygdala—the part of the brain often referred to as the "home of fear or emotion"—and has noted that changes in PAG activity occur even when you are placed in nonthreatening situations or are attending to mundane tasks like comparing alphabetical letters to each other on a computer screen.

Predicting Uncertainties

Feldman Barrett theorizes "that we don't go through life constantly detecting threats and reacting with flight-or-fight circuits. Rather, brains operate mainly by prediction, not reaction." What she says really happens is that, instead of your brain choosing to fight or fly, it assesses the situation, compares it to what it already knows or establishes new biases to base future assessments on, and provides you with the best actionable solution, which *could be* to fight or to fly (Feldman Barrett, 2024).

To put that in perspective, when you overthink, you put your brain in a perpetual state of heightened alertness. This rewires your connections, reroutes brain messages, and trains your brain to continually search for solutions to innumerable unknowns. Understandably, this process of constantly reducing uncertainty is mentally and physically exhausting, and it can be a very costly expenditure of your metabolism, pulling vital resources away from body systems that regulate mental and physical health and reallocating them to futile contemplation. Hence, those nasty psychosomatic symptoms pop up along with potentially dangerous diseases and disorders.

Your emotions play into this as well. Some of the things you overthink are not as frivolous as a theoretical hermit life; many are reenactments of past traumas and fears of future catastrophes. You might even start off with a pleasant mental ramble about the serenity of living alone in the wild but end up dreading that if you choose that lifestyle, you'll be the only human left on the earth after the inevitable global destruction that's already starting to occur and that began when your boyfriend left you and how you hated him after that, but once the world ends and you find yourself very literally single, you'd give anything to have even that big, stupid jerkface back... You'll feel everything from peace and joy to fear and anguish, and you'll keep your mind and body in a constantly jacked-up state.

Training Your Brain

Dr. Amishi Jha, an associate professor of psychology at the University of Miami and director of contemplative neuroscience at the school's UMindfulness initiative, brings the conclusions of Davidson's and Feldman Barrett's work together by assuring us that, because the brain is malleable, yes, it gets changed by our thoughts and feelings, but it can also be transformed for the better. She says you can take matters into your own hands to intentionally train your brain to rewire its neural pathways—you *can* stop overthinking.

Jha explains that emotions can have a detrimental effect on brain shape and function. Worries can keep you awake, fears can prevent you from taking progressive action, and the sum of all feelings can lead to debilitating disorders. However, consistent mindfulness equips you with powerful tools to identify negative thought patterns and emotional triggers—as well as inhibitors—and enables you to actively shift your focus away from them, helping you reclaim the power those problematic emotions have taken from you.

Some research suggests that mindfulness may even be able to improve age-related cognitive degeneration. Jha explains that the thicker the brain material is, the healthier it is. As you age, your brain tissue naturally thins, resulting in frequent forgetfulness and difficulty learning new skills. Jha points out that mindfulness prevents this thinning and says that long-term practitioners' brains actually look healthier and younger than those of their non-practicing peers.

In addition to retaining brain thickness, a group at Harvard found more density in the gray matter of the hippocampus (responsible for emotional control and memory storage) and less gray matter in the amygdala (responsible for fight-or-flight, stress, and fear management), resulted from the prolonged mindfulness study they conducted. The "good" section of the brain got bigger and thicker, and participants who reported feeling less stressed showed shrinkage of the amygdala! This means that mindfulness can keep your mind sharp *and* lessen the weight of your burdens. You don't have to eliminate external life stressors in order to reduce stress—although I'm sure that helps—mindfulness can do it for you by tempering the brain region that handles your reactions to them (Seaver, 2023).

What It Is

Mindfulness can lead to better cognitive control, which can help regulate all those emotions, tensions, and memories that your overthinking stirs up, and it can level out your mood too. So what is this magical method?

Mindfulness is "an intentional state of focused, nonjudgmental awareness of the present moment" (Seaver, 2023). Much like a gym session exercises your muscles, mindfulness methods effectively work out your brain, improving memory, attention, and emotional regulation. And, like regular physical exercise makes your body parts more accustomed to and more capable of performing certain actions, regular mindful workouts help your brain learn what to expect from various circumstances and be better able to handle all the uncertainties it encounters throughout each day.

Many mindfulness techniques require you to focus on the moment, notice what you experience, and redirect your focus if it strays. Jha equates that to a brain pushup. Now, I'm no gym rat, but I have seen the effects of regular physical activity on my body; regular mental motions like "brain pushups" can only yield positive results.

When you practice mindfulness on a consistent basis, your mind is literally changed. The moral of the story is this: Practice mindfulness techniques to shape your brain into a better-functioning, better-prepared, better-at-predicting outcomes, more efficiently responsive tool that can assess any situation without having to spin its wheels round and round in overthought to the point of mental and physical exhaustion.

In the next sections, we'll learn more about this impactful activity and put a mindfulness plan in action.

Common Myths and Benefits

Before I really looked into it, if someone suggested mindfulness to me, I brushed them off. I thought it was some new-agey thing, and I wasn't interested. I admit I bought into a bunch of the myths and misconceptions and cast judgment before I educated myself. What a mistake! There's nothing mystical or mysterious about it; to the contrary, it's very practical, convenient, free (for the most part), and, most importantly, effective.

Let's bust some myths and conquer your doubts about this beneficial practice:

- Myth #1: Mindfulness is no different from meditation.

    - Truth: Meditation is just one possible activity. The goal of mindfulness is not to silence the mind but to make it aware of your present experience. This can be achieved in a number of ways, like while walking, while sitting and breathing, *or* while meditating.

- Myth #2: Mindfulness is a Buddhist practice that conflicts with other religions.

  - Truth: Though taught by Buddha, no spiritual ideologies are involved in mindfulness. The goal, again, is to calm the mind, to be attentive to your circumstances with an air of care and concern.

- Myth #3: Mindfulness means clearing the mind of all thought.

  - Truth: While that can be incorporated into the practice, it is not what mindfulness aims to do. You will still have thoughts, and you will still hear mental chit-chat, but that internal talk will be sharply focused and highly concentrated in an effort to keep the mind on the topic of your present surroundings and the situation you are in at that very moment.

- Myth #4: Mindfulness means instant happiness.

  - Truth: Not necessarily. As Toni Bernhard of *Psychology Today* (2014) puts it, "The present moment is not always a pleasant moment." If your "right now" is right after you were reprimanded by your boss or had an argument with your spouse, the present moment may not be a happy one, but it can provide you the opportunity to make peace with the current state of your life, whatever that may be.

- Myth #5: Mindfulness is just taking time to relax.

  - Truth: You will likely be more relaxed after a mindfulness session, but there's more to this technique than just propping your feet up in a recliner. This myth is comparable to saying yoga's just the stretch and yawn you do when you crawl into bed. Like yoga works the body, mindfulness *works* the mind. During mindfulness practices, you actively and intentionally focus on the present moment, capture and proactively redirect wandering thoughts, and learn to recognize your thought tendencies in order to better manage them in the future.

Mindfulness benefits anyone who practices it, from daycare workers to emergency responders and from test-taking college students to new moms. In fact, recent studies have shown the benefits of mindfulness extend from pregnant moms to their babies, who "later showed less negative social-emotional behavior than the babies of less mindful women" (Hendriksen, 2018). What benefits can you expect to receive from this practice? Let's find out below:

- **Less stress and anxiety:** Chronic stress-induced anxiety is a growing concern, but researchers have confirmed that mindfulness reduces this angst without the worries of pharmaceutical side effects, is cost-effective (usually no costs at all), time-effective (takes little time and can be done whenever you want, no appointments necessary), and has little stigma surrounding it (unlike seeing a therapist or taking medication).

- **Fewer depressive symptoms:** Not only does mindfulness reduce depression, but it also helps prevent future episodes from occurring. Mindfulness-based cognitive therapy (MBCT), a combination of cognitive behavioral therapy (CBT) and mindfulness-based stress reduction (MBSR), is an eight-week program that is particularly effective in this area—as effective as antidepressant medications (Kuyken et al., 2015).

- **Improved overall well-being:** Consistent mindfulness practice has been shown to improve the effects of type 2 diabetes, rheumatoid arthritis, lower back pain, psoriasis, and fibromyalgia (Cash et al., 2015). It also helps you deal with illness and move on post-recovery. It can be a catalyst to motivate you to get regular checkups, pursue physical activity, and improve health habits.

- **Better emotional regulation:** Because mindfulness helps you identify your feelings, it also helps you be more aware of the feelings you experience at any given moment, thereby enabling you to rein them in and manage them effectively.

- **Stronger memory:** Mindfulness may improve your memory. As we discussed earlier in this chapter, it physiologically thickens the gray matter in your brain's hippocampus, which is the region responsible for memory storage. And as we learned, the thicker the brain, the healthier it is! So the next time someone calls you thick-headed, take it as a compliment.

- **Improved relationships:** Mindfulness is a practice of acceptance without casting judgment. As you learn to acknowledge and accept aspects of your own self, you also tend to apply this to other relationships and become more welcoming of others' flaws.

- **Sharper cognition:** Mindfulness requires the active participation of several cognitive abilities, including focused attention, redirecting thoughts, and dismissing interfering thoughts. As Dr. Jha noted in her research, practicing these things regularly actually trains your brain to do them better, and as Dr. Davidson proved, such persistent practice shapes and reshapes your brain to improve its functionality.

- **Less overthinking:** When you practice mindfulness—when you do Dr. Jha's brain pushups—you focus, notice, redirect. This trains your brain to pay attention to the thoughts cycling through it, alert you to ones that are unhealthy or unhelpful, and cut those destructive thoughts off and throw them in the trash before they get the chance to spin in circles.

Before we dive headfirst into mindfulness mind workouts, let's clear up some confusion about mindfulness and meditation.

How Mindfulness and Meditation Differ

Mindfulness and meditation are both effective means to calm your mind, settle your emotions, and improve mental focus, but they can be used together; these are two distinct concepts.

Let's start with basic definitions:

- **Mindfulness:** We've already mentioned that mindfulness involves intentional focus on the present moment. One of its most well-known proponents, Jon Kabat-Zinn (2023), defines it as "the awareness that arises through paying attention, on purpose, in the present moment, non-judgmentally." The key term here is "present moment."

- **Meditation:** This is a practice in which you focus your mind on a specific thought, or perhaps an activity or event, "to train attention and awareness, and achieve a mentally clear and emotionally calm and stable state" (Shapero et al., 2018).

The main difference between mindfulness and meditation is that, while mindfulness arrives at a calm state, that's not its primary intent; that is, however, the end goal of meditation.

A few other variances are also worth noting:

- Mindfulness does not necessarily include meditation. There are many other means of achieving mental awareness in the present moment.

- Meditation often incorporates repeated mantras that are not essential to mindfulness methods.

- Mindfulness can be practiced regardless of religious orientation and is not specifically a spiritual activity.

- Meditation, most closely associated with Buddhism, can be utilized in other belief systems by centering your focus on your spiritual devotion.

- Mindfulness can be done in a variety of ways, many of which are loosely structured and can be practiced in almost any setting.

- Meditation usually takes place in a structured setting with less flexibility than mindfulness sessions.

- Mindfulness helps you arrive at a state of mindful awareness.

- Meditation aims for a state of steadied peace.

Mindfulness and meditation can be practiced independently of each other. However, both benefit your mental and physical health and improve your overall well-being.

How to Start and Sustain Your Mindfulness Practice

Ed Halliwell, a leading mindfulness instructor in the UK, softens the straightforward definitions of mindfulness we've discussed so far. He describes the practice as a way to tune in to what we experience in mind and body "with a warm-hearted curiosity and learning and acting on what we discover—with the intention to live life as fully, wisely, and compassionately as possible" (Pattemore, 2022).

I like that! It kind of gives me the warm fuzzies. That reminds me of my psychology teacher from high school, Mr. Nelson. He was a hoot! And he could read his students as if he'd written our stories himself. When we studied the work of psychotherapist Claude Steiner and learned about stroking egos, giving people the cold pricklies, and receiving warm fuzzies, Mr. Nelson wore a special tie for each lesson. The strokes tie was light brown and had a picture of a dog being petted; the cold, prickly one had all these blue, gray, and white spiky, ice balls all over it set on a silvery background; and the warm fuzzies—my favorite—had a peachy background that was covered in smiling, furry little critters in browns and oranges that looked like they could jump right off the tie and snuggle with you. I always hoped Mr. Nelson was wearing that tie when I passed his classroom on the way to dreaded chemistry because it always perked me up and chased away the cold pricklies that awaited me in *that other class.*

Warm fuzzies are sentiments, actions, and behaviors that bring you peace and joy. They help you forget about those nasty old cold pricklies that make your heart race, fill you with fear, and chill you to the bone. For some reason, it seems the cold pricklies are the ones that capture our attention when we overthink. The good news, though, is that mindfulness can help you restore that tranquility once again.

Jon Kabat-Zinn, PhD, is the founder of the Center for Mindfulness and its Stress Reduction Clinic at the University of Massachusetts Medical School. He is known as one of the most influential teachers in the mindfulness movement, and his nine pillars or nine attitudes of mindfulness set the standard for all forms of this practice (Kane, 2024):

- **Be nonjudgemental:** Observe what's in your mind and what's happening around you without deeming any portion good or bad. Whatever you notice simply is as it is.

- **Have a beginner's mindset:** Look at the world with the eyes of a child and the fascination of seeing it for the first time. Find amazing in the ordinary.

- **Let go:** We tend to want to hold on to warm fuzzies and dump the cold pricklies. That's only natural; however, once the good and the bad have been acknowledged, they both need to be released and just observed for their having been.

- **Accept things as they are:** If you desire to change something, you must first accept it for what it is. Only then will you be able to move beyond it.

- **Be patient:** Things rarely happen according to your desired timeframe. Change, growth, and healing all take time, and you need to allow those moments to pass—or arrive—when they will.

- **Be non-striving:** Forcing things won't make them happen any faster. Hold your intention—your goals, your mindfulness, your meditation—without trying to take matters into your own hands.

- **Trust:** Have trust in yourself and in your intuition. Maintain boundaries but honor your feelings and rely on your instincts.

- **Be generous:** Give freely of yourself and devote time and energy to the welfare of others.

- **Have gratitude:** The old saying to "have an attitude of gratitude" may seem cliche, but it is sage advice that withstands the test of time. Grateful people tend to have less stress, lower anxiety, fewer bouts with depression, and general satisfaction with life. It's great to celebrate the big things in life, but don't overlook the little things, as they can add up to great joy.

Embrace one of the above attitudes and start your mindfulness practice. The list is in no particular order, and it doesn't matter which pillar you choose because they are all interconnected. Choose one you'd like to work on, and it will have residual benefits on the rest.

Mindful meditation, journaling, and yoga are some simple activities to get you started. Here's a good overview of these three options:

- **Mindful meditation:** Meditation involves focused reflection or contemplation about a particular subject, thought, or emotion. When partnered with mindfulness, it utilizes breathing techniques, stillness, and sensory awareness to become more in tune with your body, mind, and soul. Mindful meditation is known to enhance sleep, increase attention span, reduce cognitive decline, lower anxiety, lessen depression, manage weight, and improve chronic conditions.

- **Journaling:** Writing down thoughts in a journal is a good way to process experiences. By writing them out, you mentally work through them. It can help you release things you've been holding onto, and it can also help you track your triggers.

- **Yoga:** Many people choose yoga for its low-to-no costs, relative simplicity, adaptability, and convenience. There are many variations to accommodate different body types and agility factors. One method you can even do while sitting on a chair! Yoga is known to relieve anxiety—and the nervous system in general—tame the fight-or-flight response, strengthen the respiratory system, and promote relaxation.

When you commit to mindfulness practice, don't feel like you should master it right away. It's called a "practice" for a reason. Allow yourself time to get used to the exercises, and soon enough, they'll feel natural.

Practices to Try

If you are new to mindfulness practices, you might feel a little awkward focusing so much attention inward and upon yourself, but it's okay. Be gentle with yourself. Be kind and patient with your progress. Acknowledge what you feel. That's part of the process!

First, commit a specific block of time to mindfulness each day. Maybe begin with small sessions that last only 10-15 minutes and gradually increase to about 30 minutes a day over a 2-week period. Don't pressure yourself; that would be counterintuitive.

Below are several beginner-level exercises for you to try. Give each one a whirl to see which seems right for you:

- **Body scan:**

  - Lie down on your back in a quiet space where you won't be disturbed.

  - Starting at your crown and slowly working your way all the way to the tips of your toes, notice the sensations your body experiences. Stay on each area for one full minute before moving on to the next.

- **Mindful walking:**

  - Put on your comfiest cross-trainers and head outside.

  - You don't have to walk fast but move at a steady pace, taking in everything your five senses pick up. What do you smell, see, hear? And how does this physical motion make you feel?

- **Mindful meditation:**

  - Sit in a chair or on a cushion with a good but relaxed posture in a quiet place where you won't be disturbed.

  - As you breathe, notice each inhale and exhale, feel your lungs expand and empty, and hear the sound of air moving through your nose or mouth.

  - Soften your visual focus. Let your eyes lower, but don't close them. Simply allow whatever is before them to exist.

  - Notice your arms. Let your arms hang loosely by your sides, or place your palms on your thighs.

  - Notice your legs. If you're on a chair, place your soles flat on the floor; if you're on a cushion, fold your legs comfortably in front of you.

  - If your mind wanders, don't make a sudden attempt to stop it, but gently rein it in and direct it back to what you're feeling in the moment.

  - When you're ready, end the session by lifting your gaze and slowly taking note of the sights and sounds around you. Notice what thoughts you are experiencing and what your body is feeling.

- **Alternate nostril breathing:**

  - Sit comfortably with your legs crossed on a cushion on the floor.

  - Take your right thumb and press it against your right nostril. Then, inhale deeply and slowly.

  - Release your thumb and press your left ring finger against the left nostril. Exhale slowly and deeply, taking longer to exhale than to inhale.

  - Keeping the ring finger on the left nostril, inhale slowly and deeply.

  - Release the ring finger and place the thumb back on the right nostril. Exhale slowly and deeply, again taking longer to exhale than to inhale.

  - Repeat several times until you feel calm, less stressed, and more present.

- When you're done, press your right hand against your right knee and then your left hand against your left knee.

- **Engage the five senses for five minutes:**

  - Sit in a comfortable place, like on your front porch or in a neighborhood park.

  - Set your handy timer for five minutes.

  - Look, listen, smell, touch, and taste all the things that are around you. Attune to the present moment.

- **Mindfulness-based stress reduction (MBSR):**

  - This practice combines mindfulness meditation and yoga and varies by the individual participating in the activity. It follows no set steps and is not scripted but is performed in a manner that best suits you. It focuses on

    - commitment to the requisite lifestyle change that is necessary for dedicated mindfulness practice.

    - emphasizing individual effort, motivation, and regular

meditation practice even when you don't feel like doing it.

- perceiving the experience as a challenge and not a chore so that it is done in a spirit of adventure in living, not as work (Ackerman, 2024b).

Positive Psychology published the following mindfulness schedule as suggested by Dr. Amit Sood, chair of the Mayo Mind Body Initiative (Ackerman, 2024a):

- **Monday:** Pay attention throughout your day to things you are grateful for and express that **gratitude** in your journal or meditative contemplation.

- **Tuesday:** Notice those around you who may be hurting in some way and show them **compassion** as you encounter them.

- **Wednesday:** Accept yourself for who you are and extend that **acceptance** to others without trying to change them.

- **Thursday:** Consider your life's **purpose** and generate awareness of where or in what you find **meaning**.

- **Friday: Forgive** yourself for anything you've been begrudging yourself for, including perceived failures and what you think are illegitimate fears, then extend that forgiveness to others for any wrongs they have committed against you.

- **Saturday: Celebrate** all the joy in your life—however big or small—and celebrate the lives of others too.

- **Sunday:** Through awareness, meditation, or prayer, spend time in **reflection**, looking back over the past week, month, or year, or perhaps on some other specific period of time.

A recent study found mindfulness practices—MBSR in particular—to be just as effective for treating anxiety disorders as the popular pharmaceutical antidepressant drug escitalopram (Hoge et al., 2022). If your habitual overthinking has pushed your anxiety, stress, and patience to your limits, put some mindfulness practices to the test and provide your mind and your body with a natural way to restore and improve your overall well-being.

Chapter 4:

Rewriting Your Mental

Scripts

Overthinking is not a disorder, disease, syndrome, sickness, short circuit, neurosis, psychosis, or figment of your imagination. It is all in your mind, though. Well, sort of. Your thoughts are definitely internal, and they tend to stay that way unless you choose to audibly express them. But that doesn't mean overthinking is an imaginary problem. It is, however, a habit. Believe it or not, you are able to control it, just like any other habit you want to make—or break.

Establishing something as a routine requires continuous work and practice. Putting an end to one also takes intentional, persistent effort.

One way to challenge overthinking is to develop a conscious awareness of your thoughts. When a thought comes to mind, and your mental gears start spinning, stop to consider if that thought is productive. Will following that train take you to a destination or merely send you in circles? If it's intrusive, consider what evidence you have to back it up. Is it valid and worth your time to ponder it, or is it a falsehood and distraction? Training your mind to question these thoughts interrupts the cycle and shifts your focus. Over time, you can replace the habit of rumination with more constructive thinking patterns.

In this interactive chapter, we will explore different tools and techniques you can use to find your calm, become fully immersed in the present moment, and regulate your nervous system.

What Is Your Inner Dialogue Default?

Until just a few years ago, I thought everybody heard voices in their head or at least *a* voice—their own. I've always been able to hear my thoughts. I *thought* that's what *thoughts* were. As I type this, I hear myself reading it inside my head. My lips aren't moving, and no one can hear me. I'm *thinking*. But not everyone has this ability!

According to Dr. Kyle Killian (2023) of *Psychology Today*, only about 30–50% of people can hear their thoughts. That means the majority of people either don't have this internal dialogue at all or only encounter it on rare occasions. My mind was completely blown when I first learned of it. *How do other people think?* I wondered as I began to wander down rabbit holes. I could not imagine a silent mind. *That must be blissful! They don't rehash awkward conversations, awaken themselves at 3:30 a.m. with what they* should have said *to someone the day before, or get stuck on a song. Luckies! But, again, how do they think?*

Killian explains that many rely on visual imagery and memories of events to fill that quiet void, and others may think out loud, either speaking audibly or moving their lips silently. In his more than 40 years of study, Dr. Russell Hurlburt, a professor of psychology at the University of Nevada, Las Vegas, "concludes that inner speech is just one common form of thought, along with inner seeing, feeling, sensory awareness and unsymbolized thinking— in which a concept isn't necessarily attached to words or other symbols." He suggests that most people utilize a combination of thought forms when internally contemplating something (Williams, 2022). Everyone processes information, works out problems, and makes plans all in their minds too; it's just not necessarily done with internal words. That got me wondering further: *Does everyone have an inner voice?*

Your inner voice—not to be confused with inner dialogue—is essentially what you think of yourself. Imagine if you could step outside of your physical being for a moment and observe "you." The judgments you would make on those observations are your inner voice. It's supposedly an objective perspective, but it's rarely an accurate one.

Your inner voice—also referred to as your inner critic—can be nice. It can act like a loving friend, reassure you of all your positive attributes, and tell you how pretty you are. Or it can be mean. It can beat you down like a bully with insults, tell you how stupid you are, and convince you that you're doomed to failure. Dr. Małgorzata Puchalska-Wasyl of John Paul II

Catholic University of Lublin, Poland, categorizes the inner voice into four characteristics (Williams, 2022):

- **Faithful friend:** This voice is thought to be the most common. Caring and kind, it encourages you with positivity and gives you virtual pats on the back.

- **Proud rival:** This one is a competitive spirit that high-fives you but coaches you to do better.

- **Ambivalent parent:** This one's tough because it packs a punch of criticism into each offer of love and support.

- **Helpless child:** This is the most negative, often leaving you feeling powerless and desperately seeking support and encouragement.

Experiments performed by Hurlburt and Dr. Charles Fernyhough, a professor of psychology at Durham University in the UK, utilized fMRIs to compare deliberate inner speech—thoughts you are aware of "saying," like adding and subtracting numbers while trying to balance your bank account—to spontaneous inner speech—unintentional internal messages, like, "You're not good enough to get that job promotion," that your inner critic may hurl at you. They found that deliberate thoughts originated in the brain's left hemisphere, which is where speech production takes place, and spontaneous thoughts occurred in regions of auditory perception. In other words, when we "hear voices," we are listening rather than talking (Hurlburt et al., 2016).

This is why, when the negatives "speak" louder than the positives—in whatever form you "hear" them—it weighs you down with undue stress. So your inner critic may say things, but your inner self is taking it in and believing it like a child soaks up whatever their parents say to them (good or bad). It actually increases rumination because you constantly question those assessments and worry that they're true, and it can lead you into a downward spiral of belief that you have no worth.

Yes, even people who don't hear their thoughts can still be prone to both a negative inner voice and overthinking. They may replay scenes in their minds or picture events happening as if watching a film on a movie screen. Anyone can be plagued by the *habit* of thinking, rethinking, ruminating, wondering, and mentally wandering after a topic and its tangents to the point of mental and physical exhaustion.

How do you gain control over your inner voice and rewrite the script of that internal dialogue or mental screenplay? Puchalska-Wasyl advises that you pay attention to those thoughts, identify the dominant voice, and observe how its messages make you feel. She suggests that knowing which voice is guiding you can help you understand how to reframe your thoughts.

Results of the Hurlburt-Fernyhough study support Pchalska-Wasyl's idea, as they indicate that "turning spontaneous thoughts into a deliberate, more positive

[one] may help turn an inner critic into an inner coach, by transforming passive opinions into more active advice" (Williams, 2022). That's a complicated way of saying it will help you turn that frown upside down!

"That sounds great," you say, "but how do I actually *do* that?" I'm glad you asked!

1. **Listen intently:** Whenever you catch an unintentional thought popping up, stop what you're doing and tune in. If necessary, excuse yourself from a meeting, politely remove yourself from a conversation, or tell your spouse you have to go to the restroom. Go somewhere quiet with no interruptions, and pay attention to what you hear. You may need to practice actively listening to other people before you master this technique with your inner dialogue.

2. **Be curious:** Don't just hear with your internal ears; follow the trail to see where it takes you. When you reach a destination, stop and analyze what you've observed and resist the urge to overthink. Question its relevance. Determine if it was truthful. Was it just an illusion? What feelings did you experience?

3. **Write it down:** Journal the internal discourse you experience. Record the thoughts, the times and dates when they occurred, and what was happening in your life at the time. Then, write

down the answers to the questions posed in the previous step.

4. **Take a step back:** Take a breather. Practice mindfulness. Do some yoga. Take a walk. Clear your mind.

5. **Review the discussions:** Open that journal and read what you've been experiencing. Create a chart that lists positive chatter on one side of the page and negative speech on the other. For each positive, add another encouraging thought. For each negative, write down a counter-truth.

6. **Refute with truth:** Next time you hear positive inner dialogue, embrace it, but the moment something derogatory enters the conversation, stop it in its tracks. Pick up that chart you created in the previous step, and replace the lies or the hurtful statements you just heard with the ones you wrote down to counter them.

7. **Refuse to be a victim:** Resolve not to allow your inner voice to rule your life. Your mental and physical health—and your relationships, by extension—depend on it. It may sound strange, but you need to establish boundaries with your self-talk and take ownership of your thoughts, words, and actions.

Journal It

Cathy Hutchison of Your Visual Journal (2023) says journaling should be purposeful, and the way you go about it should be determined by what you want to get out of it. For self-improvement, you may ask yourself questions, set goals, and record what you learn. Therapeutic journaling should include freewriting, exploring feelings, and contemplating the reasons for feeling those emotions.

Journaling is great for those overthinking moments when you rehash a conversation or project how scenes would have gone if you'd said *this* instead of *that*. Just write it down like an actual script, recording the banter between you and your "characters." Hutchison says journaling is also an effective way to rewrite your internal dialogue. In this case, the part of you is your listening ear, and the other "character" is your inner voice. Jot down what you hear and what you say back. With practice, the conversations will become more fluid and congenial.

Cognitive Restructuring

This therapeutic technique helps you recognize negative thinking patterns that interfere with daily life, disrupting relationships and discounting achievements. These thoughts can often lead you into overthinking cycles, but cognitive restructuring (CR) puts a halt to that by deconstructing those harmful thoughts so you can reorganize them in a more accurate way.

CR is a key technique in cognitive behavioral therapy (CBT), which has proven to be a successful treatment for anxiety, depression, and personality disorders, among other conditions. Often, people who participate in such programs experience cognitive distortions, which are skewed ways of viewing the world, such as catastrophizing, black-and-white thinking, and overgeneralization. CR helps you transform such maladaptive thoughts into helpful ones by changing the way you view circumstances, enabling you to change how you feel toward those events. CR requires you to monitor your inner self, question your assumptions, and gather evidence to support or dispute those thoughts. Once you assess these aspects, you can generate alternative viewpoints that will provide a more positive outlook and a less critical inner critic.

Avoid Self-Sabotage

Self-sabotage is a nasty way to treat yourself. It often occurs when you're looking forward to doing something, but you have big doubts, shaky nerves, or a vicious inner voice telling you you've made a bad decision. What happens is you get ready, and you take the classes, buy the equipment, or learn to dance—whatever this new opportunity requires—and then you don't do the homework, get the wrong tools, or spin yourself into a tizzy on the dance floor till you're too dizzy to twist the night away at the People Without Partners community center old-fashioned sock hop.

Or worse. You've got 10 minutes to perfect your presentation before you present it to the board, but instead of sharpening your speech, you offer that valuable time to the overthinking gods and spend those final 10 minutes catastrophizing. It probably started when your proud rival inner voice said, *You can do this! Someone else could do it better, though.* The more it rambled about what could be better, the stronger points you should have included, and the great reception it could have if you had only researched the information more thoroughly, the deeper into fear and panic you fall as you become certain you're doomed to fail. *I mean, yours is fine, but if you'd put this line in there instead of that one, the chief shareholder would probably jump for joy instead of fall asleep leaning on his hand.* Then, just like that, you're called to the meeting. Because you *didn't* prep for the previous 10 minutes, and you *did* overthink, you sabotaged your potential and flopped the performance.

Speaker and author Alyce Cornyn-Selby (n.d.) defines self-sabotage concisely: "Self-sabotage is when we say we want something and then go about making sure it doesn't happen." And the funny thing is, you usually try to blame someone or something else for the occurrence. In the board meeting example, you might think the members were just a bunch of closed-minded jerks, or perhaps your assistant didn't edit the PowerPoint well enough, or the boss didn't give you enough time to prepare. While outside factors may have played some role, it comes down to what you did yourself to lock in your missteps, and you need to own that responsibility.

There are a number of reasons for self-sabotage:

- You have self-imposed limits on how much success and love you allow yourself to have, so you set yourself up to fail when you reach that limit.

- You're humble and don't want to take all the glory for yourself, so you fail in order to allow someone else to have success. Ironically, this works out to be more prideful than generous: You think so highly of yourself that you *know* you'd do a knock-their-socks-off job, so you offer it to someone else who "needs a chance."

- You have low self-esteem and don't believe you deserve success or good things.

- You fear the changes success brings, even though they're good things that you actually want.

When you face decisions, you have a very brief amount of time to choose between self-advancement or self-sabotage. Since it's common to run on autopilot, you may not even realize the choice you've made until you're in the middle of the mental action. To give your brain a fighting chance at choosing the right path here (which would be the one leading away from destruction), take some time to challenge your beliefs.

Look at that list above. Can you relate to any of those descriptions? Can you add to the list? These views could be what's holding you back and what's keeping you from achieving the success you not only seek but also deserve.

Visualization Is a Powerful Healing Tool

Walt Disney (n.d.) was right when he observed that "imagination has no age," and his contemporary, Albert Einstein (n.d.), understood that "imagination can take you anywhere." Visualization is a mental exercise in which you *imagine* some future happening the way you want it to as if it were happening right now, today. To participate in this practice, you can be a child or a child at heart! We talked earlier about your inner voice; consider this your inner eye. Look at your situation through the lens of your deepest desires, and *see* those dreams fulfilled.

Visualization involves each of the five senses to direct your subconscious toward the desired result. When used consistently, this practice can train your brain to view that end goal as having already been achieved. You do this in two parts: envisioning the desired outcome and envisioning the steps you must take to get there. The theory is that what you focus your attention on and proactively work toward is more likely to become your reality (Moe, 2021). It can work positively—say, to acquire a job promotion—or negatively—as with the board meeting presentation example in the previous section.

Cognitive behavioral theory, the foundational basis for cognitive behavioral therapy, postulates that thinking influences behavior and vice versa. It actually incorporates feelings into a middle position between the two. While feelings do not get changed directly, they are affected by how the thoughts and behaviors impact each other. Visualization is a source of manipulation to bring the three aspects into a balanced and desirable alignment that will help you reach your goals, attain what you desire, and improve your mental well-being.

Below are the basic steps to practice visualization:

- Engage all five senses and write down in full detail what it is that you want. Some people like to create a vision board and either draw or paste images that represent those desires. Set this board in a prominent place where you will see it frequently throughout each day. Also, write your goals on index cards and read them when you wake up each morning and before you go to sleep each night.

- Think about how you would feel when that vision becomes reality. Referring back to cognitive behavioral theory, involving your feelings will manipulate your thoughts and behaviors into cooperation and make you more likely to act.

- Learn all you can about your goal and the steps required to get there. You may need to take a class or do some research to enable you to physically work toward the desired result.

- Understand that there may be setbacks. Don't be defeated by them, but learn from them and grow.

- Set aside at least 10 minutes twice a day to practice visualization. Just close your eyes and imagine what you desire as if it were the present reality. See it, hear it, smell it, taste it, and touch it in your mind and fully engage your subconscious.

Another visualization technique is color breathing, in which you assign a color to a positive emotion and while performing deep breathing exercises, envision that color washing over you and filling your body, washing away all negativity. Guided imagery is also helpful. For this exercise, you sit somewhere comfortable and quiet, close your eyes, and, while performing deep breathing exercises, imagine yourself in a place where you are calm and at peace. Engage your senses; feel a soft breeze or smell fresh meadow air. Imagine peace as you inhale and expel tension with each exhale.

Visualization is a simple but powerful method you can use to boost mood, improve decision-making abilities, progress toward your goals, and break the overthinking habit.

Make a Habit of Gratitude

Visualization helps you embrace future achievements as if they were today's reality, and mindfulness keeps you centered in the present moment. Maintaining a "now" mindset enables you to acknowledge and appreciate what you have and reduces the frustration caused by contemplating what you lack. It replaces envy and greed with humility and generosity and opens your heart to gratitude.

Maintaining a consistently grateful mentality and regularly expressing gratitude bring peace of mind, relieve anxiety, reduce depression, increase optimism, improve relationships, and elevate overall well-being. To make gratitude your habit—and possibly replace that nasty habit of overthinking—anchor yourself in the present moment, look for good in the little things, work through each of your senses and notice something to be grateful for, and breathe deeply and clearly as you bring joy in and send dissatisfaction out.

Keep a running log of the positive things you observe each day. Place the list beside your bed and read through it morning and night. Express gratitude to your loved ones and to others you encounter. Keep it at the top of your to-do list, and make sure you check that box every day.

Chapter 5:

Embracing the Present and

Letting Go

A lot of overthinking is done over the difficult experiences you've gone through in your past. Whether they are the result of ancient or recent history, emotional scars reopen easily, and when you dwell on them, they remain raw and exposed. Every time you cycle back through an emotional injury, you hurt yourself. Even if the person who inflicted the harm is no longer in your life, when you ruminate about the situation, you allow the offender to keep causing you pain.

Putting the past in its place is a choice—so is holding on to it. It's time for you to choose to move forward, acknowledge what has happened, but ultimately let it go. It's the only way to truly heal.

Putting the Past in the Past

Everything that has happened in your past has contributed to the person you are today. Both the good and the bad have shaped you and influenced your cognitive, social, and emotional development. How you handle what you've gone through determines whether you stagnate or grow. The best way forward is by learning from your experiences without getting stuck on them and without reliving them in your head.

Think of the process as keeping your mental car in drive but periodically glancing in the rearview mirror. You want to be aware of the dangers that lurk back there, but you want to stay ahead of them and not let them overtake you again. Keep moving forward; don't get stuck in the historic muck, or you'll become immobilized. Your wheels will spin, but you'll get nowhere.

It's challenging, and it may take a heavy emotional toll, but letting go of past pains releases burdens you don't need to carry anymore and leaves you with a sense of freedom and a newfound hope.

Here's what you need to do:

- If you haven't already done so, distance yourself physically and emotionally from the person who inflicted the harm.

- Give yourself permission to address those old wounds. Allow yourself to face them, but limit yourself to the amount of time you spend there. You want to recognize what they are without reliving the moment.

- Permit yourself to feel. This exercise will likely stir up emotions you've shoved aside. You might become upset, but it's okay. Let them flow out of you so you can stop holding them inside.

- Be kind to yourself. Do not beat yourself up or get angry with yourself for not having gone through this process before. Don't think you *shouldn't* still feel the things you do or that you *should've* done [fill-in-the-blank].

- Allow yourself to forgive the offender. Forgiveness does not mean forgetting what happened. It simply means drawing the situation to a close and freeing *yourself* from continued pain.

- Accept that you may never receive an apology from the other person. Your healing does not depend on their actions. What matters is that you put the event in the past and move forward.

- Bring yourself back to the present. What happened is over and done. It is no longer going on right now.

- Be grateful for the experience. This is a hard one, but like I said before, going through this helped shape your "you-ness." Growth is always a good thing, even if it took great difficulty to get there.

- Surround yourself with a solid support system who will encourage you, prop you back up if you stumble, and keep you moving forward.

- Seek professional counseling if necessary. There is no shame in needing help! Some past experiences may be too traumatic to fully process on your own. Therapists are trained for this. Let them give you the boost you need.

Know that healing takes time. Be patient as you work your way through each step. Celebrate the small victories as you achieve them and find joy and hope in every tomorrow.

Strategies to Improve Present-Moment Awareness

As we discussed in Chapter 3, the brain physiologically changes when you practice mindfulness. It grows new neurons whenever you learn new skills, drop old habits, or develop new ones, and heal from the emotional injuries of your past. Every challenge, every lesson, every experience rearranges the brain's synaptic connections. When you say you feel "wired" after something exciting happens, you mean it literally!

Because of this neuroplasticity, you can train your brain to respond differently to various stimuli, including the habit of revisiting old, hurtful memories. Instead of feeling overwhelmed, distraught, angry, or confused when something triggers these reminders, you can teach your brain to become relaxed, calm, clear, and relieved. It just requires some enhancements to your mindfulness practices, like those listed below:

- **Body focus:**

    - Lie down in a quiet place where you are comfortable and won't be disturbed.

    - Pay attention to how the bed, sofa, or floor feels and the way it supports your back, head, and legs. Notice the touch of the fabric on your fingers. Is it soft, rough, or smooth?

    - Now, take one slow, deep breath in and out.

    - Focus on the top of your head and work your way to the tips of your toes. This differs from a body scan in that you're working and releasing muscle groups rather than noting sensations.

    - Intentionally contract the muscles of your scalp. Hold the tension for a few moments and then release it. Work the areas around your ears and along the back of your neck as well.

○ Move to the face. Tense and relax each group: forehead, eyebrows, eyes, cheeks, mouth, lips, jaw, and front of the neck.

○ As you work your way down, feel the tingling sensations and be reminded of the work every part of your body does throughout the day. Try to leave each muscle group relaxed. Return to the ones that are resistant.

- **Listen to autonomous sensory meridian response (ASMR):** ASMR videos have become quite popular on social media, and they're easy to search for on YouTube. Their purpose is to encourage pleasure and calm by inciting a tingling sensation in the head, spine, and limbs brought on by distinct sounds. It's often mundane tones that we usually tune out that bring us to this state of relaxation, but the audio is hyperfocused on them, excluding background noise. For example, a video creator may simply open the plastic wrapper on a piece of candy and crinkle it between their fingers or phonetically zoom in on the buzz of an electric razor trimming a man's hair.

- **Feel the beat of your heart:** Sit somewhere quiet. Take a slow, deep inhale and exhale, and then locate your pulse. Use the index and middle finger of one hand and feel the inner wrist of the opposite arm, or place them on the carotid artery in your neck just under your jaw. Tune out the noise around you and focus on your heartbeat. It may seem to grow louder as you listen more intently. Continue to take slow, deep breaths in and out, and listen to your body's rhythm for as long as you like.

- **Write down what you've done:** At the end of the day, make a list of your accomplishments. They don't have to be big ones. In fact, the smaller they are, the better because it will help you see that you have been productive with your time, and there are lots of positives to be grateful for. Some days, just getting out of bed on time can be the biggest feat of the day! Congratulating yourself on getting things done can relieve a lot of anxiety and help you be mindful of how you spend your time.

These practices can remind you of the mind-body connection and promote a more grounded, conscious way of living that improves the well-being of both the mental-emotional and the physical states of your being.

Learning to Embrace Uncertainty

Fear of the unknown is a great paralyzer. And let's face it, everything beyond this very moment is unknown. You can plan all you want, and you can prepare for every thinkable outcome, but you can never know for sure what will happen next. Depending on your current situation, that can be terrifying. Actually, even if you're in a relatively stress-free time of life, you may still be nervous about tomorrow.

It's not healthy to constantly fret over what is to come, but that's precisely what many overthinkers do. *Think* about it: If you rehash an awkward conversation, you plot what you'll say *next time*. If you're up in the air about a vacation destination, you're contemplating where you *will go*. If you worry about encountering a grizzly if you *become* a hermit, you're anticipating a future event too.

A great way to overcome this tendency is to embrace uncertainty. Here's how to find the positives in any situation and discover the silver linings that are hidden in life's experiences:

- **See the glass half-*full*:** Be optimistic. Be hopeful. See the positive potential in your circumstances. Laugh off embarrassing moments and mistakes. Celebrate your successes instead of pouting bout perceived failures.

- **Demonstrate compassion and kindness:** Open yourself up to helping others. Don't focus on your own discomfort; concentrate on lifting someone else up.

- **Adjust your faulty beliefs:** Maybe you've convinced yourself that you'll fail at every new thing, so you're better off not even trying that *uncertain* new thing. Assess your current mindset and restore truth to your convictions.

- **Remind yourself of past success:** You really haven't failed at everything, have you? And I bet you have loads of talents and abilities to tackle innumerable obstacles. Look back on the things you've done well to reassure yourself of what you can do with whatever comes your way next.

- **Be curious and courageous:** Be excited about the unknown. There's lots to learn there. You might even find things you like if you are brave enough to step forward.

- **Challenge your competitive side:** See uncertainty as an opportunity to show off your strengths and build new skills.

- **Remove "what if" from your vocabulary:** "What if" will do you in. It's the ultimate dream destroyer because it works hand in hand with catastrophizing. *Hey, I have a great idea! But what if [fill-in-the-blank-disaster] happens?* And there go all your hopes down the drain.

- **Do what makes you happy:** Fill your life with joy! Go to the spa, get coffee with a friend, or read your favorite book three times in a row! Overwhelm yourself with positivity, and there will be no room for fear or doubt.

Uncertainty is inevitable, but it doesn't have to be defeating.

Learning to Set Realistic Goals and Priorities

Do you make New Year's resolutions? *I'm going to exercise every day this year! I'm going to lose 20 pounds by June. I'm going to be more organized, go out with my friends more often, write the great American novel...* How many of those have you followed through with? If you're like 80% of people, you give up by Valentine's Day (Emde, 2023). So many people fail because they either set unachievable goals or don't properly plan them out.

You've had a lot of birthdays, right? What do you do when you blow out the candles on your cake? Make a wish. Wishes require no effort. Wishes are just magical happenstance and hopes granted by genies and fairies.

Unfortunately, many people approach goal-setting like those birthday wishes: They state the thing they want the most and wait for it to happen.

If only! Sure, goals are things you really want and maybe things you need. Oftentimes, they're events or actions you want to participate in or would like to see happen in your life. Unless you're just mean-spirited, I think it's safe to say that you set goals with positive intentions, like earning a job promotion or purchasing a new home and achieving or acquiring something for your betterment—or putting an end to your overthinking habit.

It's going to take work to get there.

When you set goals, they need to be balanced. The achievement of any one goal should not be to the detriment of another aspect of your life. For example, career advancement should not sacrifice family engagement. On the contrary, they should complement each other; spiritual pursuits should enhance personal growth.

When you write down your goals,

- be realistic; choose things you are actually capable of doing.

- assess your needs; decide how this goal benefits your life and your family.

- understand your purpose; consider why this is important to you.

- get a clear vision of what you want to accomplish; imagine attaining the desired end result.

Once you have your list ready, write down the action steps necessary to achieve those aspirations. Set due dates for completing each step, and check them off along the way. As you progress, periodically reassess your goals. Make sure they still align with your vision and the action steps still apply. Reset dates if necessary, but don't give up.

With persistence and dedication, you can let go of the past, embrace your future, and move forward into a healthier, happier you.

Chapter 6:

Strategies for Long-Term Success

They say the definition of insanity is doing the same thing over and over again but expecting a different outcome. Overthinking does involve repetitive thought, and it can drive you crazy, but it is not a mental health condition. Yes, you are sane, but no, you are not achieving different outcomes—you're reaching the same non-actionable conclusion every time.

As Albert Einstein (n.d.) keenly understood, "We can't solve problems by using the same kind of thinking we used when we created them." So, constantly thinking about something can't solve the problem of *constantly thinking about something*.

In this chapter, we're going to focus on self-observation: the skill of reflecting on your choices, attitudes, beliefs, and behaviors in an effort to bring awareness to your self-defeating habits. These are the things that aggravate your anxiety, compound your stress, and send your emotional state into overdrive, confusing cognition and contributing to poor physical health. We'll give you techniques to discover what is driving you, and then we'll explore ways to calm the nervous system back down and achieve a satisfying equilibrium in life. You'll find that rewiring your mindset and regulating your emotions and nervous system are the secrets to reducing, controlling, and getting rid of anxiety, catastrophizing, and overthinking.

The Healing Art of Self-Observation

Self-observation is an individual activity. No one can lead you through it because no one else is inside your mind. You and all the marvelous facets of you are the only inhabitants there.

As we talked about in Chapter 4, you have an inner voice, and it can sometimes speak with numerous intentions that contradict each other. Yes, you may have an argument with yourself inside yourself. It may not be internally audible; you might sense a conflict of emotions or battle indecision. When you observe yourself, you give no one and nothing but yourself your full attention while you listen to and watch your mindsets and behaviors to discover what drives your compulsive patterns.

All you need for this exercise is space, stillness, silence, and you.

One article I read compared self-observation to bird-observation, or bird-watching. Birds are anxious little critters that don't stay in one place too long. They're pretty boisterous, and they definitely don't hesitate to speak their minds or act on impulse. I honestly don't know if they think at all, but they do go through the same motions all the time, much like you do when you overthink.

Like old-time photographers used to say, "Watch the birdie!" My neighborhood is home to a pair of sandhill cranes—we affectionately call them Lucy and Ricky because they're redheads like Lucile Ball. I say it's "home," but they act like they own the place. They casually walk down the middle of the street. Sometimes, they stroll along the sidewalk, but if they want to cross to the other side, they take their grand old time. If a person, animal, or vehicle approaches, they jump and flap and squawk at them, and whoever or whatever it is has to back off and wait for the birds to go on their way. Though the cranes are not an apex species, they continuously behave like they are. Lucky for Lucy and Ricky, they're protected in this state, but if they weren't, I have a feeling their jump-flap-squawk dance would rarely end happily. Laws keep these birds safe, but you must learn to rein in your repetitive thoughts and behaviors in order to stop your mind from putting itself in the street of harmful habits.

Below are five simple steps for practicing self-observation:

1. **Ssshhh.** Be quiet. In your busy life, finding a moment of silence can be challenging, but you need to carve out time for quiet reflection. Tell your inner voice to shut up! Turn off the radio, television, devices, and anything else that makes noise, buzzes, or jingles, and isolate yourself in a room apart from people, pets, or other

distractions. Find a space where you can be alone. If you can't find a quiet space in your home, try a peaceful corner of a library or a secluded bench at a park.

2. Once you have found your quiet space, **let go** of what you would normally be doing, and don't allow yourself to think about what else you *should be* doing. This right now is what you *should be* doing, nothing else. It is time to let go of anything else that might be occupying your mind. Letting go doesn't mean ignoring responsibilities; it means prioritizing your well-being. Allow yourself the freedom to relax and just be. Just settle down and allow yourself this moment.

3. **Do nothing.** Don't fidget. Don't squirm. Don't force yourself to think on any particular topic. This may seem daunting initially, especially if you are used to being continually active or engaged. Close your eyes so you have no visual distractions, and just tune in to what's going on inside. The point of this exercise is not to force your mind to think of specific topics but to allow thoughts to come and go freely.

4. As you sit in silence, begin to **observe** your thoughts and feelings. Like meandering through an aviary to identify various birds and pay

attention to their different colors and songs, turn your vision inward and see what memories flutter by. Note the feelings that are attached to them. Listen to any thoughts that arise. Don't respond or react; just observe. Reflect on your behavior over recent days and recall how you interacted with others, performed your job, and related to your family members. Stay in this sanctuary until you feel you've perceived all there is to behold. Then, slowly open your eyes back up and return to the present moment.

5. The final step is to **write** down your insights. Writing is a powerful tool to gain clarity and understanding. What images popped into your mind during your reflection? Were there particular thoughts that stood out more than others? What tones or attitudes did you perceive? What insight did you gain? What did you learn about yourself? What areas of your life could you improve upon? Reflect on these questions as you write. This process is not just about recording what happened during your quiet time; it is about understanding yourself better.

How can you apply the knowledge you gained from this exercise to your conscious moments in daily life? Regularly practicing this internal assessment will help you understand your convictions, know why you respond to people and events in certain ways, and be aware of your triggers. From there, you can pinpoint the areas that need to be tweaked.

Regulating Your Nervous System

The autonomic nervous system controls your unconscious responses and determines whether your body should go on the defensive or just chill out. It consists of two distinct branches:

- The **sympathetic nervous system** handles sudden, stressful situations. It regulates the fight-or-flight response and signals the body to take protective and defensive action for survival. Cortisol and adrenaline are released to increase heart rate, blood pressure, and breathing to prepare the body to work if it needs to confront or escape someone or something—like if you need to run away from that bear by your hermit cottage.

- The **parasympathetic nervous system** handles recovery and relaxation. Activities like yoga, deep breathing, and meditation signal it to bring your heart rate back into a regular pattern and settle the body into a state of calm.

When your nervous system is out of whack, the sympathetic system remains on high alert, and the parasympathetic doesn't get the chance to help you unwind. Anxiety remains high, blood pressure stays elevated, and you feel overwhelmed and powerless even after a legitimate stressor is removed—like after the bear has returned to its den. When your nervous system is dysregulated, you continue to feel scared, uncomfortable, and on edge, and you experience physiological discomforts as well, like chronic pain and illness.

Dr. Linnea Passaler (2023), a surgeon and clinician with Heal Your Nervous System, says the nervous system "is the foundation of our lived experience, connecting our body and mind, regulating our emotional and mental state, immune system, and every other body system." It not only involves our whole being, but it also regulates how we interact with other beings, even allowing for spiritual connections.

According to Passaler, this interconnected system is built upon four pillars:

1. **Body:** This includes all the physiological aspects of your physical body, its operating systems, and cellular structure. The respiratory system enables you to breathe, allowing oxygen to enter your bloodstream. The circulatory system pumps this oxygen-rich blood throughout your body. Each part of your body has a role, and when you take care of your physical health, you enable these systems to work well.

2. **Mind:** The mind encompasses the thoughts and emotions that shape your daily life as well as all of your internal, non-tangible workings. This includes your feelings, how you reason, and your ability to make decisions. Self-awareness is a major component of your mental landscape that allows you to recognize your emotions and thoughts and respond appropriately to different situations. A healthy mind requires effective coping strategies. For example, journaling can help you understand your feelings better. When you write down your thoughts, you can reflect on them and gain clarity. Mindfulness and meditation promote mental wellness by encouraging you to focus on the present moment, thereby reducing stress and anxiety. Talking to someone about your feelings, whether a friend or a therapist, and verbalizing your thoughts can diffuse emotional turmoil and help you build strong mental resilience.

3. **Connection:** This refers to your relationships, how you relate to others, and how you participate in society and the general community. Humans are social beings, and your connections are important to your well-being. Healthy relationships provide support, love, and a sense of purpose. Spending time with those closest to you can strengthen emotional bonds and create a support network during tough

times, and participation in community activities gives you a sense of belonging. Simple gestures like a random phone call or quality time with loved ones can strengthen these connections. Effective communication skills like active listening, which involves fully concentrating on what someone else is saying before responding, shows respect and deepens the connection between you and your loved ones.

4. **Spirituality:** This alludes to your search for meaning and your need to connect with and be a part of something bigger than yourself. It can manifest in numerous ways, whether through organized religion, personal beliefs, or a connection to nature. Engaging in spiritual practices can offer comfort and insight into your life. For many, attending religious services creates a sense of community and belonging, encourages shared values, and fosters a supportive environment. On the other hand, individual practices like meditation or spending time in nature can enhance your spiritual experience and evoke feelings of wonder and gratitude. It is also helpful to explore your personal values and beliefs. Ask yourself what you stand for or what gives your life meaning. Engage in reflective practices to clarify these thoughts and take time to ponder life's big

questions to achieve personal growth and satisfaction.

Overall well-being is found in the balance of the body, mind, connection, and spirituality. Each aspect complements the others, creating a holistic approach to living a fulfilling life.

Healing the nervous system requires you to attend to all four of those aspects. You can't just treat the symptoms of one and expect them all to fall in order, and there is no quick fix. Regulating your nervous system in a healthy way is a lifelong journey. You need to maintain an awareness of your mental and physical states. The self-observation exercises we discussed in the last section are great for this! You also need to learn and practice healthy coping mechanisms and work to heal the negative effects of chronic dysregulation.

Here are some practical ways to calm your nervous system and restore it to a functional state:

- **Relive happy times.** This does not mean to ruminate or put the memory reels on repeat, but it does mean to visualize something that has brought you pleasure, like a serene day at the beach, a decadent dessert, or an exquisite art installment. Neuroscientist and mental health expert Caroline Leaf says, "When you visualize a happy cluster of memories, this generates a frequency in the brain that overrides the negative frequency the toxic stress caused and calms down the nervous system" (Estrada & Lucas, 2024).

- As Peter Pan advised, "**Think of a wonderful thought**, any merry little thought" (Fain & Cahn, 1953). Recall happy memories, joyful conversations, or silly childhood songs. Replace negative thoughts with positive ones, and if you struggle, try putting those negative ideas to the tune of an upbeat song to take the air right out of its sails.

- **Try some deep breathing exercises**. Slow, deep breaths let the brain know there's no need for urgency and help the body to calm down after a real or perceived threat. Ten rounds of box breathing is a quick and easy way to settle the nervous system. Simply breathe in for four counts, hold it for four counts, breathe out for four counts, and hold that for four counts.

- **Pause and apply the 30–90-second rule** to balance the brain and body before responding to any interaction. Take 3–5 slow, deep breaths, inhaling to fully expand the ribs and lungs and exhaling to empty them completely. Then, scream into a pillow to literally blow out your frustrations. And finally, do a physical action like a couple of yoga stretches or a few quick burpees.

- **Relax under a weighted blanket** to send proprioceptive input to the brain. This gentle pressure improves the awareness of your body's position in the space around you and effectively lowers the heart rate.

- **Eat.** Don't stress eat! Have a snack of healthy fats, like avocados, nuts, or fatty fish, to keep the myelin layer surrounding nerve cells healthy. Think of it as fluffing your nervous system's pillows.

Practice these techniques and do them often to restore balance and maintain a healthy nervous system that functions optimally no matter what's going on around you.

The Aim Is Not To Be Calm 24/7

You don't want to completely subdue it because the nervous system triggers the natural reflexes and activates bodily functions that preserve you from harm. You don't want it so relaxed that you have no qualms about giving that grizzly a bearhug, but you also don't want it on hyperdrive and being so on edge that you live life barricaded inside a safe room, inside a safe house, inside a safe compound, never setting foot out the door.

Equanimity is a psychological term that refers to the mind and body's ability to work together to remain steady and calm amid life's twists and turns. In contrast to neuroticism, someone in a state of equanimity maintains composure in uncomfortable situations instead of becoming overwhelmed by fear and anxiety. It requires nervous system regulation and borrows a bit of insight from stoicism in that it encourages detachment from adversity and acceptance of things beyond your control.

Epictetus (n.d.), the ancient Greek Stoic philosopher, observed, "We cannot choose our external circumstances, but we can always choose how we respond to them." Choosing not to respond to every stimulus is a sign of a healthy nervous system.

Below are several practical strategies to help you reach and maintain this state of holistic well-being:

- **Practice daily mindfulness meditations** to preserve a sense of calm in tense situations. You don't need specialized training to get started; simply find a quiet spot to sit comfortably. Breathe deeply a few times to settle in. Focus on your breath, noticing the way it feels as you inhale and exhale. If your mind starts to go off in a different direction, gently put your focus back on your breathing. You can start with just five minutes a day and gradually increase the time as you become more comfortable.

- **Set aside time for self-reflection** to assess your mental and emotional well-being. Maybe create a quiet space in your home that's just for you where you can think without distractions. You might want to set a specific time each week, perhaps on a Sunday evening, to sit down with your journal and write out your thoughts and feelings about the past week. Ask yourself questions like how you felt during different moments, what made you happy, and what challenges you faced.

- **Lead a healthy lifestyle** that consists of regular physical activity, nutritious eating, sufficient rest, and quality sleep. Aim to incorporate at least 30 minutes of exercise into your daily routine. This could be a brisk walk, cycling, or dancing in your living room. Eat a balanced diet that includes vegetables, fruits, lean proteins, and whole grains. Make sure you take time to unwind in the evening and limit screen time before bed to improve your sleep quality.

- **Express gratitude** for everything in your life, including the trying times that help you grow. You might start a gratitude journal in which you list three things you are thankful for each day. These could be big, like a supportive friend, or small, like a delicious meal. Focusing on what you appreciate shifts your mindset and helps you see the positive even in difficult situations.

- **Embrace challenges** as learning opportunities and not as threats to your success or contentment. When faced with a hurdle, take a moment to assess the situation. Ask yourself what you can learn from it and how it can help you grow. For instance, if you are learning a new skill and find it difficult, remind yourself that struggle is part of the learning process. By viewing challenges positively, you can build resilience and confidence.

- **Utilize Jin Shyin Jyutsu**, the ancient Japanese art of finger pressing, when you're in a stressful moment and cannot step away from it immediately. Simply wrap the thumb and fingers of one hand around the thumb and consecutive fingers of the other; hold each for a minute or two before progressing to the next digit; then repeat with the other hand.

- **Build meaningful connections** with friends, family, or coworkers. Start by reaching out to someone you haven't spoken to in a while. You could schedule a lunch or simply send a message to check in. Engage regularly with others to build trust and deepen relationships. You might also want to join clubs or groups that interest you, such as a book club or a sports team. The more support you have, the better you'll feel emotionally.

- **Go outside.** Take a walk in the park, relax on a porch swing, or sip a cup of tea on the balcony. Going outside is a wonderful way to clear your mind, refresh your spirit, and enjoy nature, and being in natural sunlight helps your body produce vitamin D, which is vital for overall health. Try to make it a habit to spend some time outside every day.

- **Soak up the sun.** Protect your skin from damaging rays, then spread out a blanket in your yard, at a local pool, or a nearby beach, and take in the sun's warmth. The cozy conditions will warm your mood, and the dose of vitamin D will do you good too!

- **Say *no* more often.** Lighten your load and give yourself free time. It's easy to feel overwhelmed by the many requests we receive from others. Recognize that you don't have to accept every invitation or task that comes your way. Start by assessing your current commitments and determining which ones are truly important. Practice politely declining requests that do not align with your priorities and gain back time for relaxation and personal projects.

- **Do things for *you*.** Participate in activities that promote creativity and leisure. Make time each week to do something you enjoy outside of work and responsibilities. Give yourself a break from daily pressures and allow yourself to relax and recharge. It's important to find something that brings you joy and fits into your lifestyle.

- **Listen to music** and sing along to lift your spirits and relax. Music has a powerful effect on emotions and can be a great way to express yourself. Create a playlist of your favorite tunes and set aside a few minutes each day to listen and sing, whether in the car, cooking, or just relaxing at home.

- **Play with your pet!** Research has proven that having a pet lowers stress and anxiety, reduces blood pressure, lessens depression, decreases loneliness, and makes you feel loved and happy (Marie, 2022). If you don't have one, get one! If you don't want that responsibility or are unable to own one, visit a friend who has a pet, stop by the pet store and ask to hold a hamster, or volunteer at a shelter.

Slow down and enjoy your life. Adopt an improvement mindset, include regular self-reflection, and adjust your strategies as often as necessary, and you will successfully balance your emotions and revitalize your overall well-being.

Chapter 7:

Cultivating Emotional

Intelligence

Emotional intelligence (EI)—also referred to emotional quotient (EQ)—is the set of skills you possess to recognize, name, and regulate your emotions and to identify and understand those of others. Having a strong EI helps you build compassionate relationships and make decisions that align with your personal goals and values.

Psychologist, journalist, and author Daniel Goleman did not establish the theory of EI; however, he did make it popular with the public with the release of his 1995 book that was simply titled *Emotional Intelligence*. His interpretations of EI quickly spread to administrative and executive business offices and revolutionized not only how the corporate world interacts with clients but also how they assess potential hires. Academic systems around the world have also incorporated EI curricula into their educational programs.

The concept of EI really took off in the 1990s as researchers became curious why people with high intelligence quotients (IQ) excelled in areas of knowledge but did not always find success in social, personal, or worldly pursuits. On this realization that people with "book smarts" don't always have "street smarts," psychologists John Mayer and Peter Salovey coined "emotional intelligence" to represent this underlying skill set, categorizing EI characteristics into four components:

- Being aware of your own emotions on a nonverbal level.

- Managing your emotions, controlling them, and being emotionally flexible in changing circumstances.

- Empathizing with others on an emotional level by identifying and understanding what they feel.

- Creating and maintaining relationships, developing social skills, cooperating in teamwork, and working through conflict.

Goleman added a fifth category: motivation. This is the influence emotional factors have over the choices you make, goals you pursue, and amount of perseverance you display in light of challenges.

Let's take a closer look, get a good *feel* for the subject, and learn ways to better manage your emotions.

Deconstructing Emotional Intelligence

Deconstruction is a trendy topic these days, especially in the food arena. Really! You can find recipes for anything from deconstructed eggrolls to deconstructed beef Wellington to deconstructed pecan pie and more online. I once saw a deconstructed peanut butter and jelly sandwich on a cafe menu, and I thought, *Do they just give you the jars and a bag of bread? Now they're just getting lazy!*

Well, let me assure you there's nothing lazy about deconstructing emotional intelligence. Not that it's exceptionally difficult to swallow in its entirety, but it does digest more easily when we take it one bite at a time.

Let's first understand the link between emotions and overthinking. In Chapter 5, we talked about how the unknown is a major stressor. Humans have an innate need to control what happens in their lives. But because so much of life is unpredictable, and because your command over any particular aspect is limited and dependent upon other people and variable circumstances, you might feel helpless sometimes. A perceived loss of control can lead to fear of the unknown, and fear of the unknown can lead to obsessive thought patterns that keep you desperately trying to put life in the *right* manageable order.

Fear might be the engineer, but traumatic events, childhood experiences, cognitive distortions, mental health disorders, and learned behaviors can all provide the locomotion that chugs this crazy train down the track to Distressville. By the way, to soothe your sorrows, you might want to pick up some deconstructed chocolate bars at the platform's food court—you know, a cup of hot cocoa!

Aside from the steamy mug, none of those experiences are positive, and most—if not all—can create a real emotional upheaval. You may feel sad, mad, scared, worried, hopeless, concerned, insecure, unsafe, overwhelmed, ungrateful, confused, and distraught, as well as any number of other shades of feeling depicted on Plutchik's wheel of emotions. Not only does overthinking perpetuate a cycle of futile contemplation, but it also plunges you into a pool of potentially unlimited unhealthy emotions, which then begin to negatively affect your physical health and cause you to dwell on sicknesses, treatments, and long-term prognoses, creating new worries and unknowns and fears and an overwhelming lack of control. Do you see where this is going? That's right, nowhere.

You can derail this train, though. You can deconstruct it! Remove the cars that cause you pain and get aboard a track to wellness.

Processing Emotions Thoughtfully

In Chapter 1, we talked about studies performed in the 1970s that sought to identify how many human emotions there are. Psychologist Paul Eckman determined there were only six basic ones that were common to all people around the globe, and he named them in three sets of opposing pairs: happiness and sadness, disgust and fear, and anger and surprise. You and I both know there are many more than that, right? What about nervous or hurt? Is eager an emotion? Or guilty?

Researchers at the University of California Berkeley Greater Good Science Center conducted a study to examine "the full palette of emotions that color our inner world" in 2017. They had 853 male and female volunteers view 2,185 video clips and report their emotional responses. A total of 27 distinct emotional categories were identified, ranging from nostalgic to grossed out, from contempt to triumph, and many more in between. They discovered numerous distinguishable emotions previously believed to be variants of the six basics, but they also noticed "smooth gradients of emotions" instead of the anticipated "finite clusters." This indicated an interconnection between the known emotions and how we experience them (Anwar, 2017).

More recent research finds the theory of basic emotions losing traction in favor of a potentially infinite number. Theo Tsaousides of *Psychology Today* (2023) suggests, "It all depends on how we conceptualize what an emotion is. The practical answer is that there are as many emotions as you can name." I don't know about you, but I get emotional just thinking about that possibility! And I'm not talking about one of the six. I feel a bit overwhelmed, astonished, and a little bit mortified.

How can I possibly manage an unlimited number of feelings, much less give each one a name? The thought alone is almost enough to send me on an overthinking roller coaster that could last for hours.

There's really no reason to be bothered, overcome, or exasperated, though. If you follow the helpful tips from Emma McAdam of Therapy in a Nutshell (2024), you'll feel relieved, optimistic, and hopeful to learn how emotion processing can further help in managing how you feel. Check out McAdam's O.W.E.C.A. method:

- **O: Observe** your feelings without automatically believing them or dismissing them.

- **W:** Be **willing** to recognize that feeling something doesn't necessarily make it an objective truth.

- **E: Explore** and actively seek alternative emotional responses and verify them with facts.

- **C: Choose** a path that aligns with your values and don't just react emotionally.

- **A:** Act on what truly matters to you without letting your immediate emotional state direct your response.

When feelings like bitterness surface, it's easy to believe your emotions and react harshly. Yet, if you step back to consider the emotions that are popping up, see how others may blend in, and consider how your personal history might influence your response, you can give rational thought a chance to provide clarity, and you will be able to navigate your inner emotional terrain more effectively.

Strategies to Manage and Express Emotions

Learning to recognize and work through emotions is only the first step to bolstering your EI. You also need to know what to do with them and how to express them appropriately. It's probably safe to assume that you are not an infant, toddler, or child if you are reading this book. That's good because it means you probably have a bit of experience in this area.

Eckman's six basics may expand exponentially throughout your life, but when you were a baby, those core emotions drove your survival. You were sad and angry if you were hungry or dirty, and you may have been fearful that sustenance and cleanliness wouldn't come your way. When it did, though, you were happy! And depending on what food you received, you may have also been surprised—or disgusted.

As you entered toddlerhood, you began to connect emotions to certain situations. Fear was probably dominant at this point because you had yet to realize that when Mom or Dad left your sight, they weren't gone for good. As you neared preschooler and early childhood age, you began to adopt strategies to handle tough feelings, like distancing yourself from the source of upset.

Moving into and through childhood, you developed secondary emotions. As each was validated—or invalidated—you learned to differentiate what was appropriate—and inappropriate—ways to handle these new feelings. Puberty did more to intensify emotions than to introduce new ones, and as you entered adulthood, you had a pretty good grasp on the subject.

That didn't mean you had mastered it, though. Many people continue to struggle with emotional conflicts throughout their lives—hence, overthinking exists. Some people have no buffers, while others seem hypertuned to one or two domineering feelings. Childhood experiences, life traumas, and your folks' parenting style also impact your management methods.

If you constantly struggle with being reactionary or even indecisive about how to respond appropriately to an emotional stimulus, below are some helpful steps you can take to improve your emotional management and expression:

- **Perform five acts of kindness weekly.** A 2016 study published in Psychosomatic Medicine proved the old adage that helping someone else helps you. Reduced stress-related activity, increased reward-related activity, and greater caregiver-related activity were revealed in participants' brain scans, showing giving someone else support does indeed benefit your own health (Inagaki et al., 2016). Here are some things you could do:

- ○ **Help a neighbor with their groceries:** This act may seem small, but it can make a big difference in someone's day. If you see a neighbor struggling with bags, approach them and ask if they need assistance. It can be as easy as carrying a few packages to their door. You might also offer to pick some things up for them next time you are out and about.

- ○ **Write a heartfelt note:** This can be a handwritten letter or a simple message to a friend to express your appreciation for their friendship and tell them what they mean to you. You might mention specific memories or times when they supported you. A few sentences acknowledging their kindness and warmth can really brighten their day—and yours.

- ○ **Volunteer at a local shelter:** Volunteering is a fantastic way to give back to the community and get your focus off of yourself. Local shelters and food banks always appreciate extra hands. This kind of work might involve serving meals, sorting donations, or even organizing events. If you are unsure where to start, look online for volunteer opportunities in your area or ask around in your neighborhood. Many places have flexible hours, so you can find a time that works for you.

○ **Pay for a stranger's meal:** Paying for someone else's meal or buying them coffee can create a chain reaction of kindness. This simple gesture can surprise and delight them and encourage them to pass on the kindness to someone else. You don't have to have a lot of money; even a small gesture can have a big effect.

○ **Donate unused items:** Take some time to go through your belongings and select items you don't use anymore but are still in great condition. This could be clothing you've outgrown or household items just taking up space. Deliver them to local charities or shelters that accept donations or contact organizations that offer pick-up services.

- **Go outside every day,** even if it's just for 10–15 minutes. Sunshine provides vitamin D, and fresh air is cleansing for your lungs. Observe all the sights, sounds, and feels of the surrounding environment with each of your five senses, and feel your mind and spirit lift. Here are some simple things you can do outdoors:

  - **Take a hike:** Hiking is an excellent way to enjoy nature while also getting some exercise. You could walk trails at a local nature preserve or loop the sidewalk around your neighborhood park. Be sure whichever trail you choose suits your fitness level, and check out resources like trail maps and guidebooks if you're not familiar with the terrain. Some can help you identify the flora and fauna you'll see along the way. Wear comfortable shoes and dress in layers if you anticipate changing weather conditions, and remember to bring a water bottle and light snacks like granola bars or fruit to keep your energy up.

  - **Have a picnic:** A picnic in the park is a delightful way to enjoy good food and company. It can be a simple outing with minimal planning but maximum enjoyment. You can set up on picnic tables, in grassy areas, or near beautiful views. Sandwiches, fruits, and finger foods are popular choices. If you want something other than water, bring lemonade or iced tea. Don't forget to bring a blanket to sit on, napkins or wet wipes for messes, and garbage bags for cleaning up afterward. For more fun, toss a frisbee or play card games and create some lasting memories.

○ **Plant a tree or some flowers:** Planting a tree or flowers is a rewarding activity that benefits both you and the environment. So that they actually grow well, be sure to choose plants that are appropriate for your soil conditions and local climate. If you are new to gardening, ask an expert at your local gardening center to help you get started. Water your plants regularly. It's a good idea to research the plants you're interested in. Some need more water than others. Also, provide adequate sunlight.

○ **Play a sport:** Playing sports with friends is a fantastic way to stay active while having fun. Choose a sport everyone enjoys or pick something new you're interested in learning. Pickleball is pretty popular these days! Why not give it a try? Organize a time and place to meet, make sure everyone knows the basic rules of the game, bring the necessary equipment, and challenge each other to a competition. Even if you or your team loses, you're sure to laugh together, boost your health, and strengthen your bonds with your friends.

○ **Stargaze:** Stargazing at night requires little to no preparation and can be done nearly anywhere as long as you're away from the bright lights of the city. If your own backyard is in a bright part of town, find a location with minimal light pollution like a quiet park or field. Bring along a blanket to lie down on and dress warmly if it's a cool evening. Give yourself about 20 minutes to allow your eyes to adjust to the darkness— especially if you are the one who drove to the location and are still seeing spots from oncoming headlights—and then you'll be able to see more stars. You might also want to download a stargazing app on your phone to help you identify constellations and planets in the sky. Consider bringing snacks or drinks so you can linger awhile and relax under the peaceful night sky.

- **Get offline.** Disconnect from social media, turn off the TV, and don't read a news report. All of those things are full of potential triggers that can fray your nerves, cause you to ruminate and catastrophize, and jack up your anxiety. Get the updates you need to stay aware of current events, but don't doom scroll or interact with trolls. Here are some clever offline activities:

  - **Watch your favorite old movie:** Watching your favorite old movie can be nostalgic—but the good kind that entertains you and not the bad kind that leads you down rabbit holes. It allows you to revisit characters and stories that made you feel good. Pop some corn, plop down in a comfy spot on your couch, and veg out. Add some fun by inviting friends over for a themed movie night, dressing up as the characters from the film, and preparing snacks that suit the scene.

  - **Draw or paint:** Art can be a wonderful outlet for creativity. Trying your hand at painting or drawing doesn't require you to be a professional. Start with simple materials like pencils, colored pencils, or watercolors. You can find tutorials online or simply draw what you see around you. Take a moment to sketch your favorite mug or a tree in your backyard. If you feel bold, grab a canvas and some paint. Don't worry about making it perfect; focus on expressing yourself.

○ **Have a game night:** Game nights can create lasting memories with friends or family. Board games like Monopoly, Scrabble, or Life and card games like Uno, Skip-Bo, or Phase 10 can spark laughter and conversations. You could also play video games, but try to choose uplifting ones that give you more of an old arcade experience instead of online games that isolate you in headsets and dystopian worlds. Keep snacks and drinks handy and just have fun.

○ **Go to the library:** Libraries are treasure troves of knowledge and adventure. Walk through the aisles and see what catches your eye. Do you prefer fiction or non-fiction? history? fantasy? science fiction? If you want to learn something new, look for books on topics you've always been curious about. Don't hesitate to ask a librarian for recommendations on popular titles or hidden gems. Be sure to check out the calendar for events like book clubs, author readings, or special interest classes.

○ **Do a DIY or craft project:** DIY projects can be a fun way to express creativity and make something unique. If you love to craft, make a simple project like personalized greeting cards. You can use supplies you already have at home or visit a local craft store for more materials. Follow online tutorials for guidance or let your imagination lead you. If you enjoy home improvement, repaint a room or refurbish an old piece of furniture.

- **Replace negative emotions** with compassion. This is often easier said than done, but it provides lasting inner peace. Instead of dwelling on the anger and hurt someone caused you, work toward empathy and forgiveness. Instead of allowing upset to fester, you'll find yourself freed from emotional chains. Here are some positive thoughts you can tell yourself to combat negative emotions:

- ○ **Overcoming challenges:** Life is full of challenges, and facing them can often seem daunting. However, it is essential to recognize that these challenges are opportunities for growth. When you encounter a difficult situation, take a moment to reflect on how you can overcome it. For example, if you struggle with a project at work, break it down into smaller tasks. This approach makes the challenge more manageable and allows you to build confidence as you complete each step.

- ○ **Embracing new opportunities:** Each day brings a fresh start and is an opportunity to make choices that can lead to positive changes in your life. Set a good tone for your day with your morning routine. Maybe sit down and plan or assess your goals, practice gratitude, or engage in a brief exercise session.

- ○ **Receiving support from loved ones:** Friends and family can provide encouragement during tough times and celebrate alongside you during victories. Make it a point to connect with loved ones regularly. Grab a bite to eat at your favorite restaurant, video chat for an hour, or plan to take a trip together. When faced with challenges, reach out to those you trust and share your feelings. Their support can offer a new perspective and remind you that you are not alone in your struggles.

○ **Defining your future:** Your personal history does not have to set the stage for your future. Everyone makes mistakes, and it is essential to learn from them rather than let them define who you are. Identify what knowledge you gained from those experiences and note how they can guide you toward success in the future. Set clear goals for yourself and remember that *you* have the power to shape your future with each decision and action you take.

○ **Prioritizing your well-being:** Make it job one to take care of yourself both physically and mentally. Allocate time for self-care activities like exercise, reading, mindfulness, or hobbies. Make a list of activities that bring you joy and schedule time to engage in them regularly. Don't neglect your emotional health. If something is bothering you, journal about your feelings or talk to someone you trust.

- **Laugh!** It's no joke; laughter really is good medicine. It improves your mood, relieves stress, brings oxygen into your lungs, and strengthens social bonds. It lowers the amount of stress hormones in the body, increases blood flow, and reduces your risk of heart attack. It's no laughing matter! Okay, maybe it is. Read some "dad jokes," watch a funny movie, or spend an evening at the comedy club. Laugh more; stress less. Here are some things that will tickle your funny bone:

  - **Silly animal videos:** Silly animal videos bring a smile to anyone's face. This is one of my personal go-tos! These videos usually show animals behaving in unexpected ways, and they're super entertaining. Some of them capture animals in absolutely absurd situations that somehow always seem to work out just fine. You can easily find clips on social media platforms, and longer versions are sometimes hosted on YouTube. You're likely to find yourself in a cycle of laughter instead of a cycle of overthinking!

- **Funny memes:** Funny memes have become a regular part of online culture. These amusing images or snippets of text often reflect everyday experiences like dealing with a Monday morning or the struggles of "adulting." If you don't find one that makes you giggle, create your own and spread joy to the internet! You don't have to be a graphic designer. Just choose an image that makes you laugh and add some witty text. Message them to your friends and see how they react. They'll probably send you one back.

- **Comedy TV shows or movies:** Watching comedic TV shows or movies is a fantastic way to unwind and escape from the everyday pressures of life. Sitcoms like *Friends* or *The Office* feature relatable characters and humorous situations that resonate with a lot of people, and old favorites like *Whose Line Is It Anyway?* are sure to trigger some belly laughs instead of triggering rumination tracks. You can set up a movie night of classic comedies and mix in some newer films. Watch alone or with your peeps and crank up the laugh factor.

o **Hilarious childhood memories:** Awkward moments from childhood might tempt you to overthink, rehash embarrassing times, and wish you could disappear from those moments, but some make for the best stories, and those are the ones that not only make your heart swell but also leave you laughing. Everyone has experienced a cringe-worthy feeling at some point, whether it's tripping over your own feet during a school play or saying something embarrassing in front of your crush. These moments remind us that we all make mistakes, and laughing about them can help us take life a bit less seriously. Think back to your childhood and try to recall a particularly entertaining experience. Maybe you had an embarrassing haircut or wore mismatched clothes to school. Share these stories with your friends and get them to share their own. You'll all find comfort in knowing that others have felt the same way, and it will diminish the feelings of devastation you get when you ruminate. This sharing experience can actually be therapeutic.

○ **Puns and wordplay:** Using clever language or double meanings to create humor often elicits groans and giggles simultaneously. A lot of them that make you roll your eyes are called dad jokes now, like this one: "I'm reading a book on anti-gravity; it's impossible to put down." Admit it—you snickered! Greet friends with a punny play on words or include them in casual conversations and brighten someone's day.

Give your nervous system a break. Apply the techniques suggested in this chapter each day and grow in your emotional health as you learn to develop your emotional intelligence.

Chapter 8:

Building Your Anti-

Overthinking Toolkit

So who was right, Dostoyevsky or Ray? Is overthinking a disease or just the result of an underused imagination? As we've seen, clinically speaking, overthinking is definitely not a disease, although it can lead to both mental and physical disorders. And while Ray was onto something by suggesting you don't use your creativity enough to get out of the rumination loop, I think the problem is exactly the opposite: You overthink because you come up with far too many imaginative possibilities. It's not a matter of having enough options but too many believable ones. Theoretically, if you didn't completely exhaust yourself, you could keep going and going and going like the Energizer Bunny because you might never arrive at the *right* solution or even one that is *good enough*.

Throughout this book, we've examined overthinking—being careful not to overthink it along the way—and no matter which angle we approach it from, one thing always rings true: This is a dangerous habit. You're likely familiar with what my friend calls "analysis paralysis"— running conversations, situations, memories, future possibilities (which are *probabilities* to your mindset), perceived failures, insults, choices, and, well, useless information through your mind for seemingly endless periods of time. Those moments can be triggered by the need to make a decision, regret over an argument, embarrassment from an incident, or simple things that have nothing to do with life at all, like *does thunder only happen when it's raining?*

Mental rumination is probably the most common expression of this habit, but overthinking can also manifest in other ways:

- **Reflecting:** You may spend excessive time thinking about the past and longing for days gone by.

- **Being agitated:** Your nerves are fried, you're not sleeping well, and you're very short-fused.

- **Reacting quickly and angrily:** You are on edge and jump at any words that are spoken in your general vicinity.

- **Brooding:** You focus on a negative thought so frequently that it weighs you down and keeps you in the sad, fearful, and maybe even angry and disgusted zones of the emotion wheel.

- **Depression disorders:** Long-term lingering in the depths of despair can result in persistent feelings of sadness and a loss of interest in life.

- **Anxiety disorders:** Like depression, prolonged feelings of heightened worry and angst can lead to an assortment of disorders, like social anxiety, agoraphobia, selective mutism, and panic disorder, just to name a few.

You may even find that your overthinking follows a particular motif. A 2022 study from the University College of London (UCL) studied a group of young adults aged 18–24 who ruminated in response to loneliness. They discovered five common themes in the participants' experiences (Yun et al., 2022):

- **Loneliness-related:** fearing being alone, having depressive thoughts, feeling unloved or that no one cares for or about you, feeling like you have no friend to guide or support you, thinking your family is not concerned about your well-being, believing that if you had friends you could always be around then you wouldn't have the chance to ruminate.

- **Others-related:** focusing on social relationships, obsessing over negative interactions you've had with others in the past, wondering if you are treating people correctly, wondering why people aren't treating you correctly, contemplating *Why doesn't anybody like me?*

- **Life- and death-related:** fearing death, stressing over the uncertainty of life, being unsure about an afterlife, feeling scared of how you'll die, worrying about the possible loss of a loved one, contemplating the meaning of life, wondering *Will my mom or dad still be here when I'm [a parent, retired, fill-in-the-blank]?*

- **Time-related:** focusing on periods of time like a certain event that happened in the past or a future event that you are "predicting," thinking about how you could have done or said something differently in a particular instance, thinking that you are a failure because you've "had all this time" to accomplish your goals but have nothing to show for it, promising yourself that you're going to work things out and do better.

- **Overthinking outcome-related:** having an awareness of your overthinking and stressing over how it's affecting you, knowing that your overthinking stops you from sleeping but feeling helpless because you have no off button, crying all night over a particular rumination cycle, worrying about how your habit is affecting those around you.

The majority of the participants involved in this study said that their most reliable method of handling their overthinking habit was distraction. It's actually something I applied to my own overthinking tendencies: Redirect your focus. Shift your mind from the trigger to something else. The study participants said they would go for a walk, call up their friends to hang out or participate in something that required focus and attention. We'll explore some of these ideas in the sections that follow.

The UCL research could potentially lead to targeted interventions and therapeutic treatments that could be more effective than the ones currently in use because they would hone in on precise stimuli. In this chapter, we're going to consider some strategies we haven't yet explored and help you design an approach and custom-tailor a plan that fits your specific needs.

Setting Realistic Goals, Measuring Progress, and Adjusting Strategies

I've always been a fly-by-the-seat-of-my-pants kind of girl. I only lock in dates and times for things that have to be on those dates at those times. I am not married to the clock or the calendar, and that can make goal-setting and goal-pursuing a bit tricky. In my journey to becoming a recovering overthinker, I discovered that one reason I was so successful at this habit was that it really caters to my impromptu mentality. Overthinking doesn't show up promptly for its 3:15 p.m. appointment every Tuesday and Thursday and leave when the timer dings. No, if overthinking wore pants, it would fly by the seat of them too. *Does overthinking wear pants? What would that look like? I'm picturing a speech bubble shaped like SpongeBob's friend Bubble Buddy, but instead of a top hat, he's sporting a pair of Calvins. You know? I love jeans, but they don't love me. They just don't fit me right. Even as a teen when I was tiny and lean, if I got some to fit my waist, I couldn't get them over my thick thighs, and if I got them loose enough for my legs, three of me could fit into the waist. Sweats, now they're the way to go! Easy to fly in too. Where was the last place I flew? Texas, I think...*

Oops! Right, yeah, goals. As I was saying, I've never been good with keeping structure *structured*. That is, until I had to. You know very well that overthinking can disrupt routine, barge into business meetings, and butt into private conversations. It can also crash parties, drift into your dreams, and dump buckets of ice on intimate moments. It doesn't usually inflict immediate injuries, but it definitely leaves long-lasting damage in its wake. It must be stopped, and you're going to need some discipline to make that happen.

Setting goals used to scare and intimidate me. They look really good on paper, but I'd had little success following through with them. That's not to say I failed at everything I attempted; I just didn't necessarily get from Point A to Point B in an ordered way. I always felt a sort of pride in that—I did things *my way*, baby. "They" said I had to do it their way, but guess what? My way worked just fine too. Took a little longer and had a few more dips and curves than theirs, but it still got me there. And I'm a bit more exhausted from the whole process than my friend, who followed the prescribed order, but it's okay. It's okay. I'm okay.

Let me make this easy for you: Give in now. Really. Why do things the hard way just to say you could? Let's talk about some simple ways to set goals and the most effective ways to reach them.

Reaching Your Goals Is Easier Than Reaching for the Stars

A goal is something you desire to accomplish. You probably set several basic goals every day: Get up, eat well, exercise, work, and sleep. Some people make a daily to-do list and then assess it in the evening to see how productive they were—or weren't. Even without a list, I bet if you were to look back over this day, you'd probably check off many things on that list, and you could probably write in a few more extras. So, if you think about it, setting and achieving goals isn't all that hard, and you already know how to do it!

The keys to goal success follow:

1. Take a deep breath in and out. Empty your mind. Shake out your limbs and roll your neck. Okay, now, take your right hand and reach it up to your left shoulder. Next, move that hand a little higher, lift it slightly in the air, and pat yourself on the back. Congratulate yourself for making the determination to take this first step toward breaking the overthinking habit and

committing to taking the necessary actions to reach success. Job well done!

2. Alright, the next step takes a little brain work, but it's not hard. Think. Stop! I forgot to tell you to focus on what you want to accomplish. Okay, go again: Think. Cue *Jeopardy!* music. Stop. Now that you know what you want, you can write it down on a piece of paper—in ink, so you can't erase it later and say it was never there.

3. Look at the goal you wrote down. Is it realistic? Is it achievable? Will it benefit you? Is it what you really want? *Yes* should be the answer to all of those questions, by the way.

4. Put a date on the calendar by which you'd like to reach this goal. Again, make sure it's realistic. Trying to stop ruminating within the next 48 hours will likely set you up for failure. You may be anxious to get on with things, but change takes time. Rushing yourself will only frustrate you more.

5. You've gotten ready, and you've committed to a goal. Now, write down every step you will need to take to get from where you are at this moment to that future destination. List as many or as few, as necessary. Break complicated ones into multiple smaller ones so you don't

overwhelm yourself with something difficult and give up because "it's too hard." Assign each milestone a [realistic] date on the calendar.

6. Each morning, look at your list. Consider what you can do to meet the next milestone. Each evening, cross the day off your calendar and reassess your game plan. If it's one of your target dates, and you met a milestone, celebrate! And when you eventually accomplish the overall goal, repeat step number one above. Give yourself a pat on the back, take a deep breath in and out, smile, and move ahead into the new you.

Set the right goals, allow yourself time to reach them, set the steps, mark the milestones, and follow through to greater happiness and fulfillment. Then, you can return to flying by the seat of your pants!

Creating Your Own Anti-Overthinking Toolkit

We've given you a lot of strategies to stop overthinking. Let's take a quick look back before we dive into some other ideas we haven't mentioned and figure out a personalized plan of action:

- Chapter 1:

    - Pause a moment to calm down so you can *respond* instead of *react* to stimuli.

    - Identify your emotional triggers and create a mental plan to deal with them appropriately when you encounter them again.

    - Do the opposite of what your emotions tell you to do.

    - Shift your perspective with cognitive defusion, acceptance and commitment therapy, or mindfulness practices.

    - Seek professional help.

    - Practice self-care.

    - Establish a routine.

    - Challenge negative thoughts.

    - Set realistic goals.

    - Limit stress.

- Chapter 2:

    - Get regular moderate to vigorous physical exercise.

- Have a mental health screening.

- Eat a nutritious diet.

- Allow yourself only a certain amount of time to overthink.

- Practice grounding techniques.

- Do breathing exercises.

- Practice yoga.

- Walk with mindful intention.

- Chapter 3:

  - Practice mindfulness techniques like those below:

    - Body scan

    - Mindful walking

    - Mindful meditation

    - Alternate nostril breathing

    - 5-senses scan

    - Mindfulness-based stress reduction

- ○ Meditate.

- ○ Keep a journal.

- Chapter 4:

  - ○ Identify the character of your inner voice.

  - ○ Journal about your inner dialog.

  - ○ Attend cognitive behavioral therapy and practice cognitive restructuring.

  - ○ Don't sabotage yourself.

  - ○ Practice visualization.

  - ○ Make gratitude a habit.

- Chapter 5:

  - ○ Put the past in the past.

  - ○ Focus on the present moment with these mindfulness techniques:

    - ▪ Body focus

    - ▪ View ASMR videos.

    - ▪ Feel your heartbeat.

- - ■ Write down each day's accomplishments.

  - ○ Embrace uncertainty.

  - ○ Set goals.

- ● Chapter 6:

  - ○ Practice self-observation.

  - ○ Restore and regulate your nervous system.

  - ○ Embrace challenges as learning opportunities.

  - ○ Utilize Jin Shyin Jyutsu finger pressing to relieve stress.

  - ○ Build personal connections.

  - ○ Spend time outdoors.

  - ○ Say *no* more often and avoid overcommitting yourself.

  - ○ Listen to music.

  - ○ Play with your pet.

- Chapter 7:

  - Cultivate your emotional intelligence.

  - Process emotions thoughtfully.

  - Do acts of kindness.

  - Get offline and disconnect from your devices.

  - Replace negative emotions with compassion.

  - Laugh.

It doesn't seem like there's much left, but we've saved some of the more creative ones till the last. Which of these appeal to you?

- **Ecstatic dance:** This might be good for you fly-by-the-seat-of-your-pants people because it doesn't stick to rigid structures. It's all about dancing freely and expressing your emotions through uninhibited movement.

- **Self-massage:** Can't afford a day at the spa? That's okay! You can loosen up your muscles, relieve aches and pains, and reduce the stress in your body yourself. Just position yourself in a comfortable, quiet place. Maybe light candles or put on soothing music to help you relax. Close your eyes if you want to. Then start by rubbing the soles of your feet. Move through the arches and heels, and then work upward along the calves, all the way to your shoulders and neck. Release the tension wherever you can reach.

- **The 3–2–8 TikTok workout:** There are two popular variations of this viral exercise plan. The first requires you to do strength training 3 days a week, Pilates and barre each 2 times a week, and walk 8,000 steps every day. The other option is to do Pilates and barre 3 days a week, strength training 2 days, and still walk 8,000 steps a day.

- **Ground yourself with nature:** Kick off your socks and shoes and barefoot it through the grass and dirt. Use your toes to grip the grass. Feel its coolness and the softness of the earth. Shake your hands to release any negative energy you've built up.

- **Repeat positive affirmations:** Make a list of positive statements about yourself and your life. They will help you combat fears with truths and give you courage and confidence to face the day. Try statements like

    - I let go of past hurts and face the future without fear.

- I release my desire to control all aspects of my life.

- I am present in this moment.

- I am learning every day.

- **Celebrate others:** Take your focus off of yourself and your own achievements or perceived failures and look at those around you. Rejoice in your sister's engagement, cheer your spouse across the marathon finish line, or raise a toast to your best friend's job promotion.

- **Throw away your worries, literally:** Take out a piece of paper and grab a pen. Set the timer for 10 minutes, and sit down in a quiet place. List every worry, obsession, rumination, fear, or concern that's been weighing on your mind. When time's up, read over the list and pay attention to how each item makes you feel. Then, wad the paper into a ball and slam-dunk it into the nearest trash can. This physical act doesn't actually make your problems go away, but it takes away their pressure.

Personalized Action Plan

Did you know that you process an average of 6,000 thoughts per day? Overthinking rarely introduces new thoughts but recycles ones you've already considered. According to Jeff Stone of *Psychology Today* (2024), if you slow down, step back from your "noisy inner experiences," and learn from them, you can "quiet your motormouth mind."

We've provided a lot of tools to help you do just that. It's time now for you to figure out a plan that will work for you—not your best friend, not your boss, not your dog, but you specifically. Here are some things to consider that will help you sort that out:

- Remove yourself to a quiet place that is free from distraction.

- Open your journal, pick up a pen, and list aspects of your personality.

- Draw a line under that list and create a new list of all the hobbies you enjoy. Include all areas that appeal to you, like playing sports, traveling, or bicycling.

- The next list should show places you like to go that make you feel safe, secure, and unstressed.

- Next, name the people in your life who make you feel supported, encourage and uplift you, and celebrate your victories.

- Then, write down a statement that will serve as your motivation throughout the overthinking habit-breaking process. What do you want to achieve? Why do you need to do this? What changes do you hope to see in yourself?

Once you have recorded your "about you" information, revisit the various methods we've discussed throughout this book and consider which ones are a good match for the you that you described in your journal. What activities do you think you would actually do? Which ones do you think you'd stick with long enough to make a difference? Which ones would be the most effective for you personally?

Go back to Chapter 3 and look at the sample mindfulness schedule. Then, grab your calendar and pencil in a plan. Try that for one week, and then reassess the situation. Do you need to substitute any of the practices for something different? Mix things up and go again for another week. At that point, lock things in—schedule them into your calendar in ink and commit to a routine. Keep your goals and milestones in mind as you plot out your weeks, and soon, you will stop your stinking overthinking.

Tips for Friends and Family Who Are Dealing With an Overthinker, aka YOU

One of the five overthinking themes revealed by the UCL study was outcome-oriented. An example of this type of rumination is worrying about how your overthinking is affecting other people. Is your all-night tossing and turning disrupting your spouse's sleep? Is your own resulting exhaustion stopping you from participating in family activities and making your kids feel neglected? Is your frequent contemplation distracting you from your job and compromising team projects? Is your dog staring at you with drooly jowls and pleading puppy eyes because you ruminated right through its dinnertime?

While you know the heavy tolls overthinking can take on you, you also need to be aware of the harm you may be causing to those you love and who care about you. Overthinking can ruin relationships. You may be wondering how thoughts that are concealed in the privacy of your head can bother anyone else. Well, even though no one can hear your internal conversations, your speech, attitude, and behavior toward those around you can all be influenced by what you're thinking, how often you are ruminating, and the duration of time you spend in that cycle of contemplation. Let's talk about it below:

- Overthinking can lead you down the wrong path and cause you to develop faulty beliefs. This may result in your making false accusations based on what you *think* is going on when the truth of the matter is way different. My friend's ex-husband used to do this. He would get so worked up in his mind that he would convince himself a situation had occurred in a very different way than it actually had. Then he'd pick a fight with her over something that never really happened—though in his head of overthought, it had.

- Your internal overanalysis can destroy trust. If your partner is unusually quiet over dinner and insists nothing's wrong, but you run it through a few loops of your overthinking roller coaster, you may arrive at a wrong conclusion. You might think they want to break up or they don't love you anymore and then behave coldly toward them or say hurtful things. This can lead to a mutual breach of trust when, in fact, neither partner actually *did* anything wrong.

- If your overthinking habit impacts your job performance, you could face a demotion, pay cut, or worse, loss of employment, and that can have a harsh fallout on how you provide for and contribute financially to your family. Your coworkers may also lose faith in you and not trust you to perform your duties satisfactorily. Similarly, if your work requires you to interact with customers, they may perceive your lack of focus, seek assistance from other representatives, and possibly alert your supervisor.

- When you are not fully present with your partner or your children, they can feel unloved and undervalued and believe you don't think they're worthy of your time. It can inflict lasting emotional wounds and create huge rifts in the relationships that matter the most to you.

People can easily perceive when your mind is in other places, and sometimes, irreparable damage is done. Hurt feelings and broken trust could litter your life and leave you with yet another tangent to ponder, worry about, contemplate, consider, twist, turn, and chase down rabbit holes.

Until you learn to master the techniques provided in this book, break that overthinking habit, and snap out of your analysis paralysis, the people nearest and dearest to you could use some help putting up with you—I mean, patiently and lovingly supporting you.

Here are some simple strategies your friends and family members can practice to help themselves through your overthinking (Rebecca, 2023):

- **Be patient:** Yep, it's that easy! Ha! Patience may be a virtue, but it's often developed by suffering through undesirable situations, isn't it? Someone who supports an overthinker needs to remain calm and understand that this habit annoys the one who's doing it as much as it bothers them. And, although, both of you would like it to stop, that's much easier said than done. Have you ever heard of the polar bear experiment? The late social psychologist and Harvard University professor Daniel

Wegner broke ground with his revelation "that trying to suppress unpleasant thoughts actually *increases* their recurrence long-term" (Myler, 2024). In his experiment, Wegner asked participants to talk for five minutes about the thoughts that were running through their minds at the present moment *without thinking about a polar bear.* He found that they ended up verbalizing thoughts about a white bear about one time during each of the five minutes. So A) you can't just not think about something because someone tells you not to think about it, and B) thought suppression doesn't work. This leads to our next point.

- **Let you talk:** If something's on your mind enough that you start running in circles with it, maybe you should let it out—or, as Wegner suggested, free the bears. But there's a catch. Your supportive friend should encourage you to verbalize your thoughts, but only for a limited time—like around 10–15 minutes. This forces you to be concise and efficient with your words, focus on the point of your pondering, and communicate it in an effective way. It lets them in on an intimate piece of you and demonstrates to you that they genuinely care about your well-being and want to help you if you'll let them— and not just ruminate about your misinterpretations of their dinnertime introspection.

- **Listen without judging:** Your supportive friend or partner should allow you to express what's muddling through your mind without getting annoyed with you for thinking so much about that *stupid* thing or criticizing you for hanging on to something for so long because, after all, *the past is in the past*. They shouldn't think less of you for having developed this habit but should be proud of you for taking steps to address it.

- **Give honest support:** They should listen without making any judgment calls, but—and this is a big *BUT*—they should not lightly dismiss it either. They should be honest—but not hurtful—when they give you feedback, and they should communicate clear boundaries to you that they cannot just drop what they're doing and come to your rescue every time you feel pulled down the overthinking path.

- **Challenge the beliefs you're holding on to:** They should question the things you express that don't match up to what they know about your values and convictions. As we've mentioned, overthinking can result in faulty beliefs—like dwelling on your spouse's quietude during dinner to the conclusion that they hate you. They can also encourage you to think positively about yourself and prompt you to boost your self-esteem by reminding you of your good qualities, your amazing talents, and the joy you bring to them and others. They should challenge you to list the evidence to back up any flawed foibles and help you counter false concepts with truthful ones.

- **Help you focus on the positive:** Much overthinking is spent on negative ideas like doom-dreaming, predicting failure, and catastrophizing. You might spend your time ruminating about how you caught the Thanksgiving turkey on fire last year, running through each moment of that dreadful day and rolling your eyes at all the teasing and tormenting people threw at you. Your support team, though, could help you change your perspective on that memory: "Hey, we all learned that whole chickens cook up pretty well in the pressure cooker—and in much less time—and they taste just as heavenly as turkey when stuffed with dressing and smothered in gravy." And they could encourage you not to let that one bad experience undermine your future holiday feasts and festivity.

- **Encourage a creative release:** Perhaps you need an outlet for the buildup of rumination frustration. A cooking class might be a good idea, uh-hum! Maybe painting, dancing, singing, or gardening suits your passions better. Remember, Amit Ray suggested that overthinkers were being undercreative with their imaginations, so sign up to learn something new or start practicing a hobby you already know. Your friend and you can do these things together and support each other in a fun way. They could also help you find healthy coping mechanisms—like mindfulness practices, journaling, or yoga— and encourage you to do them daily.

- **They should not try to change you:** You are who you are, and your loved ones love you for *you*. They want to help you change this habit, not make you into someone else, so they need to be sure to focus on the overthinking problem without trying to compromise your convictions or coax you into becoming something or someone that you're not.

- **Help you find professional assistance if necessary:** Some emotional issues run too deep for you to process on your own, but therapists are specially trained to bring those to light and help you heal. Some forms of treatment encourage spousal or partner participation, so it's something you might be able to attend together or work on as a couple. Whichever method you choose, their encouragement will be your support as you learn to overcome your difficulties.

Breaking the overthinking habit and restoring a healthy emotional state can take time. It's important for those who are close to you to remain calm when you are struggling, extend empathy to you and what you're experiencing, and be compassionate as you learn to work through your challenges and manage your thoughts. They want you to be the best version of you, and they can demonstrate that desire through their steadfast, loving, and loyal presence.

Conclusion

Overthinking can be described as passive, futile, critical, vague, wasteful, pointless, consuming, destructive, and addictive. And I think we've seen in this book how true every one of those descriptors is! Even on the odd occasion that overthinking is entertaining, it's still a harmful habit with innumerable consequences.

As we've learned, though not a disease *or* an underuse of imagination, overthinking can lead to emotional distress, psychological disorders, and faulty thought patterns. If you allow it to continue, it can consume your mind and separate you from the important things—and people—in your life. Persistent rumination, analysis paralysis, continual contemplation, or whatever you want to call it, can leave you unbalanced and unwell, both mentally and physiologically. It can impact job performance, disrupt relationships, and leave you dealing with not only your overthinking habit but all the resulting fallout, which, by the way, is likely to make you overthink even more.

But there is hope! And we've revealed it in the pages of this book. We've helped you understand why you overthink and how to change your brain physically by practicing healing techniques. We've examined several routes you can take on this journey, and we've explored a plethora of tools to help you *stop your stinking overthinking*!

In *Stop Your Stinking Overthinking: Strategies for Quieting the Busy Mind, Letting Go, and Staying Present*, you've been given

- tips for managing, reducing, *and stopping* overthinking.

- practices that will enhance your overall well-being.

- ways to regulate your nervous system.

- tips for setting, working toward, and achieving your anti-overthinking goals.

- strategies to retrain your mind and grow empowering habits.

- tips for limiting stress and eliminating overthinking triggers.

- ways to tailor an action plan to your personal needs.

Remember that overthinking is not built into your being. It's a habit—a nasty one like picking your nose! And that means you have a choice to keep on keeping on in this burden of excessive thought or to break free, regain your freedom, and throw that boogery tissue away!

You picked up this book. That was your first step toward health and healing.

I wish you great success in your journey, and I'd love to hear about how this book has benefited you. If you feel so inclined, please leave a review on Amazon and share your experience. And if you know of anyone who might benefit from the advice in these pages, consider gifting them a copy so they, too, can *stop* their *stinking overthinking*!

References

Ackerman, C. E. (2018, February 12). *Cognitive restructuring techniques for reframing thoughts.* Positive Psychology. https://positivepsychology.com/cbt-cognitive-restructuring-cognitive-distortions/#worksheets-cognitive-restructuring

Ackerman, C. E. (2024a, August 3). *23 amazing health benefits of mindfulness for body and brain.* Positive Psychology. https://positivepsychology.com/benefits-of-mindfulness/

Ackerman, C. E. (2024b, September 17). *Mindfulness-based stress reduction: The ultimate MBSR guide.* Positive Psychology. https://positivepsychology.com/mindfulness-based-stress-reduction-mbsr/

Anwar, Y. (2017, September 7). How many different human emotions are there? *Greater Good Magazine.* https://greatergood.berkeley.edu/article/item/how_many_different_human_emotions_are_there

Anxiety disorders—facts & statistics. (2022, October 28). Anxiety and Depression Association of America. https://adaa.org/understanding-anxiety/facts-statistics

Bardo, N. (2022, January 9). Silencing your inner critic: A beginner's guide. *It's All You Boo.* https://itsallyouboo.com/silencing-your-inner-critic/

Bernhard, T. (2011, June 6). 6 benefits of practicing mindfulness outside of meditation. *Psychology Today.* https://www.psychologytoday.com/us/blog/turning-straw-gold/201106/6-benefits-practicing-mindfulness-outside-meditation

Bernhard, T. (2014, June 5). 7 myths about mindfulness. *Psychology Today.* https://www.psychologytoday.com/us/blog/turning-straw-gold/201406/7-myths-about-mindfulness

Bhandari, T. (2023, April 19). Mind-body connection is built into brain. *ScienceDaily.* https://www.sciencedaily.com/releases/2023/04/230419125052.htm#google_vignette

Brown, H. (2024, July 26). *What is emotional intelligence? +18 ways to improve it* . Positive Psychology. https://positivepsychology.com/emotional-intelligence-eq/

Cash, E., Salmon, P., Weissbecker, I., Rebholz, W. N., Bayley-Veloso, R., Zimmaro, L., Floyd, A., Dedert, E., & Sephton, S. E. (2015). Mindfulness meditation alleviates fibromyalgia symptoms in women: Results of a randomized clinical trial. *Annals of Behavioral Medicine: A Publication of the Society of Behavioral Medicine*, *49*(3), 319–330. https://doi.org/10.1007/s12160-014-9665-0

Cassata, C. (2021, June 9). 10 areas that mindfulness & meditation make us better. *Psych Central*. https://psychcentral.com/blog/surprising-health-benefits-of-mindfulness-meditation

Ceruto, S. (2024, October 23). *How overthinking in relationships can destroy your connection & how to break the cycle.* MindLAB. https://mindlabneuroscience.com/overthinking-in-relationships-destroy-connection/

Challenging negative thinking. (n.d.). MindWell. https://www.mindwell-leeds.org.uk/myself/exploring-your-mental-health/depression/challenging-negative-thinking/

Cherry, K. (2022, September 2). *Benefits of mindfulness.* Verywell Mind. https://www.verywellmind.com/the-benefits-of-mindfulness-5205137

Cherry, K. (2024, July 14). *The 6 types of basic emotions and their effect on human behavior.* Verywell Mind. https://www.verywellmind.com/an-overview-of-the-types-of-emotions-4163976

Christian, K. (2021, September 16). *What is embodiment & how can we use it for self-care?* The Good Trade. https://www.thegoodtrade.com/features/embodiment-definition/

Claude Steiner biography. (2015, August 9). Eric Berne M.D. https://ericberne.com/claude-steiner-biography/

Cornyn-Selby, A. (n.d.). *Alyce Cornyn-Selby quotes.* A-Z Quotes. https://www.azquotes.com/author/64065-Alyce_Cornyn_Selby

Davidson, R. J., & Lutz, A. (2008). Buddha's brain: Neuroplasticity and meditation. *IEEE Signal Processing Magazine, 25*(1), 176–174. https://www.ncbi.nlm.nih.gov/pmc/articles/PMC2944261/

Dibdin, E. (2022a, March 29). Need to control everything? This may be why. *Psych Central.* https://psychcentral.com/blog/why-you-need-to-control-everything

Dibdin, E. (2022b, March 31). The mental health benefits of journaling. *Psych Central.*

https://psychcentral.com/lib/the-health-benefits-of-journaling

Dina. (2019, October 31). *10 surprising exercises to improve mindfulness.* HubPages. https://discover.hubpages.com/health/Mindfulness-Exercises-You-Never-Tried

Disney, W. (n.d.). *Walt Disney quotes.* A-Z Quotes. https://www.azquotes.com/author/4000-Walt_Disney/tag/imagination

Dostoyevsky, F., MacAndrew, A. R., & Marcus, B. (2004). *Notes from underground, White nights, The dream of a ridiculous man, and Selections from the house of the dead* (150th Anniversary Edition). Signet Classics. (Original work published 1862)

Dr. Amit Ray biography. (2023, April 3). Dr. Amit Ray. https://amitray.com/amitray-biography/

Dunham, W. (2023). Scientists identify mind-body nexus in human brain. *Reuters.* https://www.reuters.com/lifestyle/science/scientists-identify-mind-body-nexus-human-brain-2023-04-19/

Eddins, R. (2022, May 4). *Working with your inner critic.* Eddins Counseling Group. https://eddinscounseling.com/working-with-your-inner-critic/

The Editorial Team. (2022, November 29). *Daniel Goleman's emotional intelligence theory explained.* Resilient Educator. https://resilienteducator.com/classroom-resources/daniel-golemans-emotional-intelligence-theory-explained/

Einstein, A. (n.d.-a). *Albert Einstein quotes.* Quotation.io. https://quotation.io/quote/cant-solve-problems-using-kind-thinking

Einstein, A. (n.d.-b). *Albert Einstein quotes.* BrainyQuote. https://www.brainyquote.com/quotes/albert_einstein_121643

Eliaz, I. (2022, September 21). *Break free from chronic stress cycle—with nature's help.* Isaac Eliaz MD. https://dreliaz.org/break-free-from-the-chronic-stress-cycle-with-natures-most-powerful-herbs/

Emde, A. (2023, June 12). *How to write your goals for a balanced life.* Lifestyle Anytime. https://lifestyleanytime.com.au/how-to-write-down-your-goals-for-a-balanced-life/

Engebretson, P. (2021, February 12). How to stop overthinking everything: Close your open question loops - i'm busy being awesome. *I'm Busy Being Awesome.* https://imbusybeingawesome.com/open-question-loops/

Epictetus. (n.d.-a). *Epictetus quotes*. A-Z Quotes. https://www.azquotes.com/quote/90291?ref= communication

Epictetus. (n.d.-b). *Epictetus quotes*. Goodreads. https://www.goodreads.com/quotes/7588248- we-cannot-choose-our-external-circumstances- but-we-can-always

Estrada, J., & Lucas, C. (2024, May 17). *10 ways to regulate your nervous system, according to a brain and behavior experts*. Well+Good. https://www.wellandgood.com/regulate-your- nervous-system/

Fain, S., & Cahn, S. (1953). *You can fly! You can fly! You can fly!* Peter Pan Original Motion Picture Soundtrack. Walt Disney Records. https://genius.com/The-jud-conlon-chorus- you-can-fly-you-can-fly-you-can-fly-lyrics

Farris, M. (2022, July 13). How to manage difficult emotions. *Counseling Recovery*. https://www.counselingrecovery.com/blog- san-jose/-feel-your-feelings

Feldman Barrett, L. (2024, August 8). Simplistic "fight or flight" idea undervalues the brain's predictive powers. *Scientific American*. https://www.scientificamerican.com/article/si mplistic-fight-or-flight-idea-undervalues-the- brains-predictive-powers/

Frontiers of the Mind. (2023, February 1). National
Institute of Health National Library of
Medicine.
https://www.nlm.nih.gov/exhibition/emotions
-and-disease/index.html#section6

Getting started with mindfulness. (n.d.). Mindful.
https://www.mindful.org/meditation/mindfuln
ess-getting-started/

Gibbons, E. (2023). The surprising benefit of
meditative walks. *Nature.*
https://doi.org/10.1038/d41586-023-01894-1

Gordon, E. M., Chauvin, R. J., Van, A. N., Rajesh, A.,
Nielsen, A., Newbold, D. J., Lynch, C. J., Seider,
N. A., Krimmel, S. R., Scheidter, K. M., Monk,
J., Miller, R. L., Metoki, A., Montez, D. F.,
Zheng, A., Elbau, I., Madison, T., Nishino, T.,
Myers, M. J., & Kaplan, S. (2023). A somato-
cognitive action network alternates with
effector regions in motor cortex. *Nature, 617*, 1–
9. https://doi.org/10.1038/s41586-023-05964-
2

Gould, W. R. (2024, March 7). *How to let go of the past and
embrace your future.* Verywell Mind.
https://www.verywellmind.com/how-to-let-go-
of-the-past-8600268

Greenfield, K. (2020, January 4). The 4-7-8 breath
technique and relaxation exercise. *The Joy Within.*

https://thejoywithin.org/breath-exercises/4-7-8-breath-technique-and-relaxation-exercise

Grover, S. (2018, July 11). Where do you store stress in your body? Top 10 secret areas. *Psychology Today.* https://www.psychologytoday.com/us/blog/when-kids-call-the-shots/201807/where-do-you-store-stress-in-your-body-top-10-secret-areas

Gupta, A. (2022, April 29). *Are you stuck in the vicious cycle of overthinking? It's risky, warns an expert.* Healthshots. https://www.healthshots.com/mind/mental-health/heres-how-overthinking-can-impact-your-overall-health/

Gupta, S. (2024, April 29). *Feeling anxious? Try the 5-4-3-2-1 grounding technique.* Verywell Mind. https://www.verywellmind.com/5-4-3-2-1-grounding-technique-8639390

Gura, S. (n.d.). *Stop struggling in your life and relationships.* Shira Gura. https://shiragura.com/

Hanh, T. N. (n.d.). *Thich Nhat Hanh quotes.* BrainyQuote. https://www.brainyquote.com/quotes/thich_nhat_hanh_591335

Harvard DCE Professional & Executive Development. (2024, January 9). How to improve your emotional intelligence. *Professional & Executive*

Development | *Harvard* *DCE.*
https://professional.dce.harvard.edu/blog/how
-to-improve-your-emotional-intelligence/

Heartwell, S. (2019, April 22). The art of conscious breathing: A powerful exercise to purify and rejuvenate the body and mind. *Conscious Lifestyle Magazine.*
https://www.consciouslifestylemag.com/breath
ing-heal-exercises-body-mind/

Hendriksen, E. (2018, October 29). The 5 biggest myths of mindfulness. *Scientific American.*
https://www.scientificamerican.com/article/th
e-5-biggest-myths-of-mindfulness/

Hoge, E. A., Bui, E., Mete, M., Dutton, M. A., Baker, A. W., & Simon, N. M. (2022). Mindfulness-based stress reduction vs escitalopram for the treatment of adults with anxiety disorders: A randomized clinical trial. *JAMA Psychiatry, 80*(1), 13–21.
https://doi.org/10.1001/jamapsychiatry.2022.3
679

Hoshaw, C. (2021, February 9). *How to calm your nervous system.* Healthline.
https://www.healthline.com/health/mind-
body/give-your-nervous-system-a-break

How to practice gratitude. (n.d.). Mindful. https://www.mindful.org/an-introduction-to-mindful-gratitude/

Hurlburt, R. T., Alderson-Day, B., Kühn, S., & Fernyhough, C. (2016). Exploring the ecological validity of thinking on demand: Neural correlates of elicited vs. spontaneously occurring inner speech. *PLOS ONE*, *11*(2), e0147932. https://doi.org/10.1371/journal.pone.0147932

Hutchison, C. (2023, September 4). How to journal | the ultimate guide. *Your Visual Journal.* https://yourvisualjournal.com/how-to-journal-the-ultimate-guide/

Inagaki, T. K., Bryne Haltom, K. E., Suzuki, S., Jevtic, I., Hornstein, E., Bower, J. E., & Eisenberger, N. I. (2016). The neurobiology of giving versus receiving support. *Psychosomatic Medicine*, *78*(4), 443–453. https://doi.org/10.1097/psy.0000000000000302

Johanson, D. (2022, February 11). *The science of sadness.* Cosmos. https://cosmosmagazine.com/health/body-and-mind/the-science-of-sadness/

Jones, H. (2023, October 2). *10 exercises that help you stop overthinking.* Verywell Health.

https://www.verywellhealth.com/how-to-stop-overthinking-7570368

Kabat-Zinn, J. (2023, December 5). *Wherever you go, there you are: Mindfulness meditation in everyday life; 11th edition.* Hachette Go. https://a.co/d/bAEQMBe

Kaiser, B. N., Haroz, E. E., Kohrt, B. A., Bolton, P. A., Bass, J. K., & Hinton, D. E. (2015). "Thinking too much": A systematic review of a common idiom of distress. *Social Science & Medicine, 147,* 170–183. https://doi.org/10.1016/j.socscimed.2015.10.044

Kane, R. (2024, February 19). *Jon Kabat-Zinn's 9 attitudes of mindfulness (+ PDF).* Mindfulness Box. https://mindfulnessbox.com/the-9-attitudes-of-mindfulness/

Killian, K. (2023, April 25). How inner monologues work, and who has them. *Psychology Today.* https://www.psychologytoday.com/us/blog/intersections/202304/inner-monologues-what-are-they-and-whos-having-them

Koehler, J. (2024, September 18). Achieving an equilibrium of the mind. *Psychology Today.* https://www.psychologytoday.com/sg/blog/beyond-school-walls/202306/achieving-an-equilibrium-of-the-mind

Kuyken, W., Hayes, R., Barrett, B., Byng, R., Dalgleish, T., Kessler, D., Lewis, G., Watkins, E., Brejcha, C., Cardy, J., Causley, A., Cowderoy, S., Evans, A., Gradinger, F., Kaur, S., Lanham, P., Morant, N., Richards, J., Shah, P., & Sutton, H. (2015). Effectiveness and cost-effectiveness of mindfulness-based cognitive therapy compared with maintenance antidepressant treatment in the prevention of depressive relapse or recurrence (PREVENT): a randomised controlled trial. *The Lancet*, *386*(9988), 63–73. https://doi.org/10.1016/s0140-6736(14)62222-4

Langshur, E., & Klemp, N. (2021, November 1). *How to make gratitude a daily habit*. Mindful. https://www.mindful.org/how-to-make-gratitude-a-daily-habit/

Lewandowski, G. (2023, March 7). How worrying and overthinking can ruin your relationship. *Psychology Today*. https://www.psychologytoday.com/us/blog/the-psychology-of-relationships/202303/how-worrying-and-overthinking-can-ruin-your

Lim, A. (2022, April 4). *Using Your Body to Express More Than Emotion*. Traditional Chinese Medicine World Foundation. https://www.tcmworld.org/using-your-body-express-more-than-emotion/

Lim, A. (2023, January 26). *The role of emotions in health and healing.* Traditional Chinese Medicine World Foundation. https://www.tcmworld.org/role-emotions-health-healing/

Lindberg, S. (2023, March 21). *How to let go of things from the past.* Healthline. https://www.healthline.com/health/how-to-let-go

Lonczak, H. S. (2020, November 17). *36 ways to find a silver lining during challenging times.* Positive Psychology. https://positivepsychology.com/find-a-silver-lining/#techniques

Mara. (2024, April 14). *How to effectively stop overthinking and enjoy life.* Important Enough. https://importantenough.com/how_to_stop_overthinking/

Marie, S. (2022, April 15). 10 mental health benefits of pets. *Psych Central.* https://psychcentral.com/health/pets-and-mental-health

Martins, I. L. (2020, July 6). How to practice positive self-talk. *Ivan Leal Martins.* https://www.ivanlealmartins.com/blog/how-to-practice-positive-self-talk

McAdam, E. (2021, July 9). *Skill #20 intrusive thoughts and overthinking: The skill of cognitive defusion - therapy in a nutshell.* Therapy in a Nutshell. https://therapyinanutshell.com/skill-20-intrusive-thoughts-and-overthinking-the-skill-of-cognitive-defusion/

McQuillan, S. (2024, June 28). What is your inner voice telling you? *Psychology Today.* https://www.psychologytoday.com/us/blog/cravings/202406/what-is-your-inner-voice-telling-you

Merriam-Webster. (n.d.-a). *Neuroplasticity.* In Merriam-Webster.com Dictionary. Retrieved October 5, 2024, from https://www.merriam-webster.com/dictionary/neuroplasticity

Merriam-Webster. (n.d.-b). *Plastic.* In Merriam-Webster.com Dictionary. Retrieved October 5, 2024, from https://www.merriam-webster.com/dictionary/plastic

Meyer, L. (2021, September 24). 5 mindful steps for self-observation. *Psychology Today.* https://www.psychologytoday.com/intl/blog/mindful-recovery/202109/5-mindful-steps-self-observation

Milbrand, L. (2023, June 29). *The 3-2-8 TikTok workout you might want to try.* Real Simple.

https://www.realsimple.com/the-3-2-8-tiktok-workout-you-might-want-to-try-7555470

Mind-body linkage is built into the structure of the brain, study reveals. (2023, April 17). *News-Medical.net*. https://www.news-medical.net/news/20230419/Mind-body-linkage-is-built-into-the-structure-of-the-brain-study-reveals.aspx

Mindfulness meditation: A research-proven way to reduce stress. (2019, October 30). American Psychological Association. https://www.apa.org/topics/mindfulness/meditation

Moe, K. (2021, June 4). 5 visualization techniques to help you reach your goals. *Betterup*. https://www.betterup.com/blog/visualization

Morin, A. (2023, November 3). *Healthy coping skills for uncomfortable emotions.* Verywell Mind. https://www.verywellmind.com/forty-healthy-coping-skills-4586742

Morin, A. (2024, June 16). *How to stop overthinking.* Verywell Mind. https://www.verywellmind.com/how-to-know-when-youre-overthinking-5077069

Most women think too much, overthinkers often drink too much. (2003, February 4). *University of*

Michigan News. https://news.umich.edu/most-women-think-too-much-overthinkers-often-drink-too-much/

Myler, C. (2024, June 4). *Stop overthinking now: 18 ways to control your mind again.* Science of People. https://www.scienceofpeople.com/stop-overthinking/

Nicks, S. (1977). *Dreams [Song]. On Rumours.* Warner Records. https://genius.com/Fleetwood-mac-dreams-lyrics

Nolen-Hoeksema, S. (2004). *Women who think too much.* Henry Holt and Company.

Online Etymology Dictionary. (n.d.). *Neuro.* In Online Etymology Dictionary. Retrieved October 5, 2024, from https://www.etymonline.com/search?q=neuro

The overthinking epidemic: Is modern society encouraging us to think too much? (2023, June 30). *A Life Well Lived.* https://www.alife-welllived.com/blog/theoverthinkingepidemic

Parker, M. (2023, May 20). *Stop overthinking: A practical guide to finding peace of mind and letting go.* OCBF Press. https://a.co/d/7ShS7iy

Parvez, H. (2024, July 13). *Cognitive behavioural theory explained.* PsychMechanics.

https://www.psychmechanics.com/cognitive-behavioural-theory-cbt-in/

Passaler, L. (2023, May 12). *Nervous system regulation: How to start regulating your nervous system*. Heal Your Nervous System. https://healyournervoussystem.com/nervous-system-regulation-how-to-start-regulating-your-nervous-system/

Pattemore, C. (2022, May 27). How to get started with practicing mindfulness. *Psych Central*. https://psychcentral.com/health/new-to-mindfulness-how-to-get-started

Pawula, S. (2021, June 13). A simple way to balance your emotions and revitalize your body. *Always Well Within*. https://always-well-within.squarespace.com/blog/2013/02/17/balance-your-emotions-and-body

Pelini, S. (2024, June 25). An age-by-age guide to helping kids manage emotions. *The Gottman Institute*. https://www.gottman.com/blog/age-age-guide-helping-kids-manage-emotions/

Ranganathan, V. K., Siemionow, V., Liu, J. Z., Sahgal, V., & Yue, G. H. (2004). From mental power to muscle power--gaining strength by using the mind. *Neuropsychologia*, *42*(7), 944–956. https://doi.org/10.1016/j.neuropsychologia.2003.11.018

Ray, A. (n.d.). *Amit Ray quotes*. Goodreads. https://www.goodreads.com/quotes/10112922 -overthinking-is-not-a-disease-it-is-due-to-the

Raypole, C. (2020, April 22). *7 emotion-focused coping techniques for uncertain times*. Healthline. https://www.healthline.com/health/emotion-focused-coping

Razdan, B. L. (2023, August 20). Training the brain to be happy. *Greater Kashmir*. https://www.greaterkashmir.com/opinion/trai ning-the-brain-to-be-happy/

Rebecca. (2023, July 19). 12 practical tips to help you deal with an overthinker. *Minimalism Made Simple*. https://www.minimalismmadesimple.com/ho me/how-to-deal-with-an-overthinker/

Reed, P. (2021, December 15). *Physical activity is good for the mind and the body*. U.S. Department of Health and Human Services. https://health.gov/news/202112/physical-activity-good-mind-and-body

Regan, S. (2021, January 18). *How to listen to your own inner voice & why it's so important*. Mindbodygreen. https://www.mindbodygreen.com/articles/liste n-to-your-inner-voice

Rice, A. (2021, October 26). Yoga for anxiety: 9 poses to try. *Psych Central.* https://psychcentral.com/anxiety/yoga-for-anxiety

Ridley, Y. (2024, February 5). How to grounded yourself: 6 grounding techniques. *Put the Kettle On.* https://putthekettleon.ca/how-to-stay-grounded-and-centered-in-life/

Russell, M. (2021, September 24). How to slow down: 20 simple ways to slow down & enjoy life. *Simple Lionheart Life.* https://simplelionheartlife.com/how-to-slow-down/

Sabater, V. (2023, June 7). *Naikan therapy: The healing art of self-reflection.* Exploring Your Mind. https://exploringyourmind.com/naikan-therapy-the-healing-art-of-self-reflection/

Sabater, V. (2024, April 8). *Seven Differences Between Mental and Emotional Health.* Exploring Your Mind. https://exploringyourmind.com/differences-between-mental-and-emotional-health/

Sander, V. (2022, November 9). How to stop overthinking social interaction (for introverts). *SocialSelf.* https://socialself.com/blog/stop-overthinking/

Santos-Longhurst, A. (2024, January 25). *What are the symptoms and causes of high cortisol levels?* Healthline. https://www.healthline.com/health/high-cortisol-symptoms#what-it-is

Schaffner, A. K. (2023, June 8). *Equanimity: The holy grail of calmness & grace?* Positive Psychology. https://positivepsychology.com/equanimity/

Schembra, C. (2024, September 5). Intelligent selfishness: How giving to others enriches your own life. *Rolling Stone.* https://www.rollingstone.com/culture-council/articles/intelligent-selfishness-giving-others-enriches-own-life-1235094815/

Schultz, J. (2020, July 24). *5 differences between mindfulness and meditation.* Positive Psychology. https://positivepsychology.com/differences-between-mindfulness-meditation/

Scott, E. (2023, October 23). *How to set and crush your goals with way less stress.* Verywell Mind. https://www.verywellmind.com/goal-setting-and-reaching-goals-3145004

Seaver, M. (2023, August 9). *What mindfulness does to your brain: The science of neuroplasticity.* Real Simple. https://www.realsimple.com/health/mind-mood/mindfulness-improves-brain-health-neuroplasticity

Seaver, M. (2024, April 26). *12 everyday habits to train your brain to be happier.* Real Simple. https://www.realsimple.com/how-to-be-happier-7485523

Shapero, B. G., Greenberg, J., Pedrelli, P., de Jong, M., & Desbordes, G. (2018). Mindfulness-Based interventions in psychiatry. *FOCUS, 16*(1), 32–39. https://doi.org/10.1176/appi.focus.20170039

Stanborough, R. J. (2023, June 5). *How to change negative thinking with cognitive restructuring.* Healthline. https://www.healthline.com/health/cognitive-restructuring

Steffen, P. R., Austin, T., & DeBarros, A. (2016). Treating chronic stress to address the growing problem of depression and anxiety. *Policy Insights from the Behavioral and Brain Sciences, 4*(1), 64–70. https://doi.org/10.1177/2372732216685333

Stone, J. (2024, October 22). Men and the hidden costs of overthinking. *Psychology Today.* https://www.psychologytoday.com/us/blog/the-souls-of-men/202409/men-and-the-hidden-costs-of-overthinking

Stress. (n.d.). Mind. https://www.mind.org.uk/information-support/types-of-mental-health-problems/stress/causes-of-stress/

Stress. (2024, May 20). Cleveland Clinic. https://my.clevelandclinic.org/health/diseases/11874-stress

Strick, M., Dijksterhuis, A., & van Baaren, R. B. (2010). Unconscious-thought effects take place off-line, not on-line. *Psychological Science, 21*(4), 484–488. https://doi.org/10.1177/0956797610363555

Therapy in a Nutshell. (2021). Intrusive thoughts and overthinking: The skill of cognitive defusion 20/30 [Video]. *YouTube.* https://www.youtube.com/watch?v=V3vhXQy48jo

Therapy in a Nutshell. (2022). Catastrophizing: How to stop making yourself depressed and anxious: Cognitive distortion skill #6 [Video]. *YouTube.* https://www.youtube.com/watch?v=bS2LPNlO07s

Therapy in a Nutshell. (2023a). Automatic negative thoughts - break the anxiety cycle 11/30 [Video]. *YouTube.* https://www.youtube.com/watch?v=lLZ-3TSoe9E

Therapy in a Nutshell. (2023b, November 9). *How to stop overthinking: Master the ACT skill of cognitive defusion 13/30* [Video]. YouTube. https://www.youtube.com/watch?v=OhNm7ZSiZls

Therapy in a Nutshell. (2024, January 4). *Emotional reasoning- the cognitive distortion that makes you emotionally reactive - anxiety 18/30* [Video]. YouTube. https://www.youtube.com/watch?v=YBzvkgA Rehg

Tsaousides, T. (2023, July 23). How many emotions can you feel? *Psychology Today*. https://www.psychologytoday.com/us/blog/s mashing-the-brainblocks/202307/how-many-emotions-are-there

U.S. Department of Health and Human Services. (2018). Physical activity guidelines for Americans 2nd edition. *U.S. Department of Health and Human Services* (pp. 8–10). https://health.gov/sites/default/files/2019-09/Physical_Activity_Guidelines_2nd_edition.p df

Vandervort, S. (2024, May 29). Get out of your head and into your body with these five practices. *The Local Mystic*. https://thelocalmystic.com/get-out-of-your-head-five-practices/

Viezzer, S. (2024, February 5). *How to improve emotional intelligence.* Simply Psychology. https://www.simplypsychology.org/how-to-improve-emotional-intelligence.html

Washington University School of Medicine. (2023, April 20). Hidden linkages: Scientists find mind-body connection is built into brain. *SciTechDaily*. https://scitechdaily.com/hidden-linkages-scientists-find-mind-body-connection-is-built-into-brain/

Wegner, D. (1990, June 1). *White bears and other unwanted thoughts: Suppression, obsession, and the psychology of mental control.* Penguin Books. https://a.co/d/iKczKER

Wegner, D. (2011, November). *Setting free the bears: Escape from thought suppression.* American Psychologist. https://dtg.sites.fas.harvard.edu/DANWEGNER/pub/Setting%20free%20the%20bears%202011.pdf

Wegner, D. M., & Schneider, D. J. (2003). The white bear story. *Psychological Inquiry, 14*(3/4), 326–329. https://www.jstor.org/stable/1449696

Weil, A. (2006, May 8). Richard Davidson. *TIME*. https://content.time.com/time/specials/packages/article/0,28804,1975813_1975844_1976433,00.html

Why laughing is good for you. (2024, August 29). Cleveland Clinic. https://health.clevelandclinic.org/is-laughing-good-for-you

Williams, C. (2022, July 4). *How to understand your inner voice and control your inner critic.* New Scientist. https://www.newscientist.com/article/mg2553 3941-100-how-to-understand-your-inner-voice-and-control-your-inner-critic/

Winzeler, M. (2020, May 27). *Calm your body and mind: A therapist's guide for nervous system regulation.* WellnessWinz. https://wellnesswinz.com/2020/05/27/calm-your-body-and-mind-a-therapists-guide-for-nervous-system-regulation/

Working out boosts brain health. (2020, March 4). American Psychological Association. https://www.apa.org/topics/exercise-fitness/stress

World Health Organization. (2022, March 2). *COVID-19 pandemic triggers 25% increase in prevalence of anxiety and depression worldwide.* World Health Organization. https://www.who.int/news/item/02-03-2022-covid-19-pandemic-triggers-25-increase-in-prevalence-of-anxiety-and-depression-worldwide

Yun, R. C., Fardghassemi, S., & Joffe, H. (2022). Thinking too much: How young people experience rumination in the context of loneliness. *Journal of Community & Applied Social Psychology.* https://doi.org/10.1002/casp.2635